T0305104

THE CLASSICAL TRADITION
IN ECONOMIC THOUGHT

The Classical Tradition in Economic Thought

Perspectives on the History of Economic Thought
Volume XI

Edited by
Ingrid H. Rima

Professor of Economics,
Temple University, US

Published for the History of Economics Society
by Edward Elgar

Published by
Edward Elgar Publishing Limited
Gower House
Croft Road
Aldershot
Hants GU11 3HR
UK

Edward Elgar Publishing Company
Old Post Road
Brookfield
Vermont 05036
US

British Library Cataloguing in Publication Data
Classical Tradition in Economic Thought. –
(Perspectives on the History of Economic
Thought; Vol. 11)
  I. Rima, Ingrid H.   II. Series
  330.153

ISBN 1 85898 141 7

Printed and bound in Great Britain by
Biddles Ltd, Guildford and King's Lynn

Contents

Contributors

William D. Grampp, Department of Economics, University of Illinois, Illinois, USA.

Paul A. Heise, Department of Politics and Economics, Lebanon Valley College, Annville, Pennsylvania, USA.

Spencer J. Pack, Connecticut College, New London, Connecticut, USA.

Andreas Ortmann, Department of Economics, Bowdoin College, Brunswick, Maine, USA.

Stephen Meardon, Department of Economics, Duke University, Durham, North Carolina, USA.

Charles E. Staley, Department of Economics, State University of New York at Stony Brook, Stony Brook, New York, USA.

Hans E. Jensen, Department of Economics, University of Tennessee, Knoxville, Tennessee, USA.

Harvey Gram, Department of Economics, Queens College, City University of New York, Flushing, New York, USA.

Mark Knell, Department of Economics, De Montfort University, Leicester, UK.

Sunder Ramaswamy, Middlebury College, Middlebury, Vermont, USA.

Introduction

Ingrid H. Rima

The great tradition of classical economics is an enduring source of inspiration for new research relating to the development of economics as a discipline. The papers presented at the twentieth annual meeting of the History of Economics Society in Philadelphia, Pennsylvania, June 1993, at the Albert H. Greenfield Conference Center of Temple University, reflect the durability as well as the diversity of classical research themes for historians of economics.

The classical tradition, broadly conceived, has developed along two quite distinct intellectual highways. The most familiar, of course, is that which may be termed 'Smithian' classicism. Its central core is encapsulated in the theory of market equilibrium operating via the price mechanism, and has been transmitted virtually intact from Adam Smith to Alfred Marshall to modern day economists. The core of its research programme which is captured in Adam Smith's metaphor of the 'invisible hand' derives from the idea of a spontaneous order that is the outcome of human action without being the product of human design.

An alternative, though less well known interpretation of classicism which can be traced back to Quesnay and the Physiocrats, has at its core the Marxian notion of social surplus. Thus the focus of its research agenda is substantially different from that of Smithian classicism. Its concern with the social surplus dictates an analysis in which the social product, the wage and technical conditions of production have already been determined. Thus, its analytical concern is to establish the conditions of *reproduction* in the sense of 'prices of production' that will allow products to just cover costs and earn profits at the 'ordinary' rate of return on the value of the capital advanced at the beginning of the uniform period of production. In its modern form the surplus approach stems essentially from Piero Sraffa's reinterpretation of Ricardian economics in his *Production of Commodities by Means of Commodities* (1960). Sraffa's contemporary followers have succeeded in articulating a research agenda which, while it is by no means the dominant paradigm, has nevertheless produced a body of research which is challenging the more familiar Smithian classicism.

Despite the familiarity of Smithian classicism, the search for understanding within this paradigm is ongoing, as the papers included in this volume will attest. The effort to reformulate, modify, extend or elaborate Smithian classicism centres chiefly, as might be expected, on various aspects of Smith's 'invisible hand' metaphor and its related philosophical notion of 'nature' and natural, including the scope for policy intervention, given the limits of human rationality. The question of inconsistency between the perspective of *The Theory of Moral Sentiments* (*TMS*) and *The Wealth of Nations* (*WN*), i.e. the so-called 'Adam Smith problem', also remains a topic of inquiry. There are also the questions relating to the analytical sophistication and consistency, especially of those parts of Smithian and post-Smithian economics that are of modern interest.

It is among the best known dicta of the classical tradition that the advantages of a market economy over a command economy derive from the limited rationality of humans. The conventional wisdom credits Adam Smith with priority in identifying and understanding the many nuances of the invisible hand metaphor. Thus there is new insight in the argument offered by William D. Grampp in his paper 'An appreciation of mercantilism', which comprises Chapter 1 of this volume, that there is a substantially greater consistency between mercantilist and classical thinking on this matter than is generally recognized. His research establishes that much of the conventional wisdom about the analytical shortcomings of mercantilist writings is mistaken, and that one cannot only construct a concept of the market from mercantilist writings, but also discern that they had an understanding of the price mechanism as well as such key economic aggregates as output, employment and the price level.

The concepts of 'natural harmony' and 'natural liberty' are prominent in both *WN* and Smith's earlier *TMS*. Given the link between Smith's emphasis on the role of nature, the presence of Stoic thought in Smith's work and thus in the classical tradition has become a research agenda in its own right. In Chapter 2, Paul A. Heise continues this line of inquiry in his paper 'Stoicism in the *EPS*: the foundation of Adam Smith's moral philosophy' by re-examining Smith's *Essays on Philosophical Subjects* (*EPS*), which were published posthumously in 1795. He argues that Smith's work 'must be read in the language of the Stoics'. The *EPS* present a Stoic model of human behaviour in which humans are conceived to behave according to 'the original principles in human nature'. Heise interprets this model as being prior and distinct from Smith's later model in which human behaviour is conceived as resulting from human faculties of reason and speech. The latter are not specifically identified until Smith's later work *WN* was undertaken, where it became an integral part of Smith's cohesive model of human behaviour that began from the philosophical grounding of the *EPS*. This is an interpretation which alters the balance of importance between human nature and the individual in Smith's work.

Spencer J. Pack's paper 'Adam Smith's unnaturally natural (yet naturally unnatural) use of the word natural', which appears as Chapter 3, examines the philosophical aspects of Smith's work, and by extension, the classical tradition, by deconstructing his use of the words 'nature' and 'natural'. Pack maintains that contrary to the conventional wisdom, Smith was not unambiguously in favour of or normatively disposed towards 'nature', or that which is 'natural', in the sense of equating it either with the discovery of God's design and/or an ideal moral order consistent with the general interests of society. His argument, supported by numerous examples, is that the words 'nature' and 'natural' are complex and often ambiguous, and that Smith did not necessarily approve of the things and behaviours he denoted as being natural or as reflecting nature.

In Chapter 4, Andreas Ortmann and Stephen Meardon address the human behaviour problem in terms which they call the 'Smith game'. The latter is a generic term for the kinds of 'hawk–dove' and 'prisoner's dilemma' games that are implicit in *TMS* and *WN*. They maintain that a game-theory approach captures the tension which arises between individual and aggregate rationality. It thus contributes toward resolution of the so-called 'Adam Smith problem' that some analysts believe exists because of the emphasis which Smith places on sympathy in *TMS*, as opposed to his emphasis in *WN* on self-interest. The incentive problem modelled by the Smith game is seen as contributing towards a reconciliation of the seemingly disparate approaches of Smith's leading works.

Smith's capability as an analytically consistent theorist is a perennial issue which Charles E. Staley undertakes to re-examine in terms of Smith's theory of wages in Chapter 5. The conventional argument is that Smith offered numerous wage theories which are not necessarily consistent. The question is whether the multiple theories – specifically the wages fund theory, the subsistence theory, the bargaining theory and the residual claimant theory – can be made consistent with one another. Staley's textual reinterpretation is accompanied by a series of graphs which are designed to show that Smith's several theories can be integrated into an analytically consistent whole that supplies a tenable explanation of wage differentials from the very short run to a nation's entire life-span.

The work of John Stuart Mill stands out as posing a substantial challenge to the efficacy of Smith's invisible hand as a universal promoter of progress for all classes of society. While he finds little fault with the power of the market as it relates to the laws of production, the matter is otherwise in relation to the laws of distribution. The famous caveat which Mill is thus led to articulate in relation to capitalism is well known. What is less well known are the 'remedies' which Mill puts forward as an alternative to the prospect of socialism. Hans Jensen's paper 'Institutionalist supports in the classical economics of John Stuart Mill', which is Chapter 6, interprets Mill's analysis, especially as it relates to the phenomenon of distribution as dependent principally on economic institutions rather than on human nature. The most important of these is the institution of private property which has become vested with a 'sacredness' in the course of capitalist development that has stultified the advancement of those who are propertyless and who have been precluded from acquiring those elements of character which educational and other institutions associated with wealth have transmitted to the upper classes. This leads Jensen to further examine the pernicious institutions that are at the root of working-class poverty and injustice, with a view to exploring what sorts of changes capitalism will require if it is to survive. The latter aspect of Mill's work, according to Jensen, anticipates the work of Adolphe A. Berle and Gardener C. Means, who are to be remembered not only as leading figures (after Veblen) in the tradition of institutionalism, but as the authors of *The Modern Corporation and Private Property*, which is among the 'truly epochal books of the 20th century'.

As the six papers encapsulated above make abundantly clear, Smithian classicism is not only alive, but its adherents are generating an ongoing flow of interpretative literature. It is, indeed, the ruling paradigm. Yet, the alternative tradition of Ricardo–Marx–Sraffa classicism has a substantial number of adherents. Krishna Bharadwaj, who was among Piero Sraffa's ablest students at Cambridge University, was a persuasive contemporary interpreter of this variant of the classical tradition until her recent untimely death. I greatly admired her scholarship and considered her a friend. Four papers were delivered as a tribute to her memory at the twentieth annual meeting of the History of Economics Society in Philadelphia. The two that are included in this volume, the first by Harvey Gram, and a second jointly authored by Mark Knell and Sunder Ramaswamy, leave no doubt that classical economics as it exists today indeed has many faces.

1 An appreciation of mercantilism*

William D. Grampp

Everie man naturally will follow that wherein he seeth the most profitt. (Thomas Smith, *A Discourse of the Common Weal of This Realm of England*, 1549)

The desire of bettering our condition ... comes with us from the womb and never leaves us till we go into the grave. (Adam Smith, *The Wealth of Nations*, 1776)

The argument of this paper is that the mercantilists and the classical economists shared certain important ideas – about how the economy actually operates, how it should operate, how it could be changed, and for what purpose the changes should be made. The propositions should be taken seriously, not simply noticed and set aside as anomalies. They invite us to think of classical economics as an extension of mercantilist ideas and of mercantilist ideas as an extension of the thinking that preceded them.

The paper is in four parts. The first is the positive economics of the mercantilists, ie., their description of how the economy operates, the market in particular, with particular attention to the ideas that reappeared in classical economics and in economic thinking down to the present. The mercantilists usually stated their positive economics when arguing for or against changing things; hence it is difficult to separate from their normative economics. In so far as the latter can be separated, it is the subject of Part II.

Both are about ideas in England from about 1500 to 1750, not about events and not about what the state or the private sector did. Such things are economic history; this paper is about the history of economics. Their relation may be interesting, important, and curious, or it may not be. In any event it is too extensive to be gone into here.

Part III describes the exceptions the classical economists made to the principle of free exchange and to its practice. The exceptions, if their source were not known, would be called mercantilist, and as likely as not called fallacies. Yet the exceptions were made by Smith and later classical economists. They appear to be anomalous because Smith is believed to have said the market economy is a naturally harmonious order that regulates itself. For the government to interfere with it is either useless or (more likely) harmful.

* This is an abridgement of the chapter of the same title in *Mercantilist Economics*, edited by Lars Magnusson and published by Kluwer in 1993 in its Recent Economic Thought Series. I am indebted to the publisher for permission to do this.

Part III argues that the classical economists, including Smith, did not give an important place in their doctrine to the idea of a natural order. If the argument is granted, it is another reason to claim classical economics was an extension of mercantilist thinking.

In the first three parts, what the mercantilists did not contribute is reported and also what the classical economists got wrong, especially Smith. The report is not a catalogue of errors, because it is not complete, and there is more attention to classical economics than to mercantilism. If this is imbalance, it may be excused because turn-about is fair play. Historians have paid much more attention to the mistakes of the mercantilists than to those of their successors. Part IV is a coda that summarizes the paper.

I   The positive economics of mercantilism

That people are self-interested and try to get as much as they can for as little as possible is stated frequently in the mercantilist tracts from the fifteenth century to those of the mid-eighteenth that were concurrent with the emergence of classical economics. The desire to better our condition which comes with us from the womb and remains until the grave, as Smith put it, was familiar for centuries before he described it. What also is interesting is that the mercantilists, like their successors, distinguished between self-interest as a fact and self-interest as a standard for judging behaviour. Most of them did not approve of letting it run unbridled. Neither did the classical economists, who did however give it a longer rein. Believing it should be given any rein at all is significant because the belief implies self-interested behaviour can be desirable. That is a consequentialist, or utilitarian, view of it, as distinct from the idea that self-interest is a right. Limit it, redirect it, even at times release it – is what most said.

A few did say that 'seeking after gain' on the market was immoral per se. John Deacon said a price should be regulated by 'equality' and Christian conscience and that if reasonable men differ about equality they should do as they would be done by.[1] His was distinctly a minority view.

The majority view entailed a market. If one claims, as most mercantilists did, that people are self-interested and about certain things should do as they wish, one then is drawn to consider what happens when they meet. The scene of the encounter is the market. The outcome is peaceful and useful because the limits of self-interest have been set down. So must the mercantilists have believed who did not say self-interest should be outlawed. The consensus on this point can be missed in the cloud of contention over other ideas. While most agreed that self-interest should be given some latitude they contended over how much and of what kind. While almost everyone agreed there should be a market and almost as many agreed the market should be regulated, they did not agree on what the regulation should be or its purpose. The classical economists, although they advocated much less regulation, did advocate some, and like the mercantilists they differed about it.

The point, in brief, is that what the mercantilists had to say about self-interest is one of the ways they anticipated classical economics.

A mercantilist tract that said much about self-interest is *A Discourse of the Common Weal of This Realm of England* (1549) by Thomas Smith. 'Every man naturally will follow that wherein he sees the most profit', he said. He put the idea to work. The output of grain could be increased by allowing husbandmen to 'have more profit by it than they have and liberty to sell it at all times as freely as men may do their other things'. That seems to endorse the universal practice as well as the principle of the free market. Actually it does not. It uses self-interest in order to achieve an end, here a decrease in the price of grain. He also favoured manipulating the market, e.g., by requiring farmers who kept sheep to keep cows also in order to increase the supply and reduce the price of butter and cheese. He said the government should induce workers to move from one place to another in order to restore the countryside which the enclosure movement had depopulated, the inducements to be free rent and cheap loans. These and other forms of intervention (e.g., prohibiting the export of raw wool) call for substantial limits on the exercise of self-interest. Moreover, it is placed in an ambiguous light by the writer's saying, 'There must be something devised to quench this insatiable thirst of greediness of men; covetousness must be weeded out by the roots, for it is the destruction of all good things.' But the ambiguity is removed (or compounded) by his asking, 'Can we devise that all covetousness be taken from men? No, no more than we can make them without ire, without gladness, without fears, and without all affections. What then? We must take away from men the occasion of their covetousness in this part.'

What he seems to have meant is that policy should utilize self-interest. Where people acting only for themselves would promote improvement, as he believed they would on a free market for grain, he urged them to do so. Where they could be induced to promote improvement, as he believed labourers could be by rent subsidies, he advocated the state's directing or modifying self-interest. He did not rule out suppressing it. If neither free pricing nor subsidizing would bring about the desired result, he advocated prohibition. He proposed an embargo on the export of raw wool in order to (a) lower its price, (b) increase the amount worked into woollen goods, (c) increase employment in the manufacture of woollens and (presumably by a multiplier effect) in the entire economy, (d) increase the population of the towns where the woollen goods were manufactured, and (e) so reverse the depopulation of the provinces. But the suppressing of self-interest was to be done with circumspection. 'For many heads will devise many ways to get something by.'[2]

Manipulating self-interest is a policy that calls for the nicely calculated less and more. It also calls for a government that is competent enough to administer it and honest enough to want to. The impartial spectator might doubt that all of these conditions could be met. He would not however say that on this point the classical economists differed from the mercantilists. They too could be unrealistic. Or fanciful. An example is Smith's (and Hume's) notion of how to check religious fanaticism (described below).[3]

The mercantilists noticed the many ways that self-interest reveals itself. What they said is as interesting and as consonant with later economics as what was said about the principle itself as the *primum mobile* of behaviour. In the anonymous *Policies To Reduce This Realme of England unto a Prosperous Wealthe and Estate* (1549), there appears the statement, 'For every man will sell his wares at the higheste price he may.'[4] Lest it be passed over as trivial, let it be noticed as the explanation of why supply curves slope upward. The author had much to say about the enclosure movement. He made it the cause of high food prices because it reduced tillage – which is to say, in the language of a later century, it moved the supply curve to the left. So also did engrossing, in the author's opinion. It was not everyone's opinion: some mercantilists believed engrossing increased competition, hence reduced prices. The author of *Policies* believed the engrossers were so few in number that they had monopoly power. One would have to say that each was correct on the assumption each made.

One would have also to say the opinion of each entailed the idea that a change in supply causes price to change in the opposite direction. In *Policies* the author deplored the attempt to lower food prices by law. 'Surely it is not the setting of low prices that will anything amend the matter. But it must be the taking away of the occasion of the high prices', the 'occasion' being a decrease in supply.[5]

Yet he could believe, just as Thomas Smith did, that some markets should be free without believing all should be. Each said the state, for the sake of its improvement, should use the self-interest of individuals, should allow it to have its way in some markets, and should restrict it in others. *Policies* advocated a tax on sheep, the intention being to limit the amount of land used for grazing and make more available for tillage. Tillage was to be increased also by allowing grain to be exported. The writer also advocated taxing people who ate meat on days when they were supposed to eat fish.

Among the other writers in whose works the idea of self-interest appears as a fact of behaviour and a force to be utilized or countered are: Bieston (1558), Hemming (1578), Malynes (1622), Misselden (1622), Petty (1662), Barbon (1690), Child (1690), North (1691), Davenant (1695), Defoe (1732), Tucker (1750), Berkeley (1751), and Postlethwayt (1759).[6] The list is not comprehensive but is long enough to indicate that the idea was known to the mercantilists. Moreover it was not a fleeting presence but the premise from which they reasoned about the nature of their world. Consider how Malynes explained the workings of a market:

> Every man knoweth, that in the buying and selling of commodities there is an estimation and price demanded and agreed upon between both parties, according to a certain equality in the value of things, promoted by a true reason grounded upon the commodious use of things. So that equality is nothing else but a mutually voluntary estimation of things made in good order and truth wherein equality is not admitted or known.[7]

The passage implies more than that self-interest directs the market. It says price is determined by the 'commodious use' (utility) of what is exchanged, that such use is something the buyer and seller estimate rather than something they know with certainty, that the estimate of each is the same, and being the same it makes the price the buyer is willing to pay equal the price the seller is willing to accept. How near the passage comes to claiming there is mutual advantage in exchange is open to some (but not much) argument. It certainly does not claim that what one person to an exchange gains the other person loses. This needs saying because the mercantilists have been charged with believing there is no mutual advantage in foreign trade.[8]

The way Malynes and others described a market anticipates some of the things said later about the operation of demand and supply. They were said more often, actually, by the neoclassicists than by Smith, the classicists being more interested in the long-run course of the economy than its affairs from day to day when supply and demand analysis is more relevant.

The mercantilists applied demand and supply analysis to the question of whether a market should be regulated and if so in what manner. Many were opposed to extensive control, a few to control of any kind, and most to particular controls of one kind or another either because the writer believed the particular market should not be controlled or because heads would devise ways to get by. Malynes was against regulating the price of goods and the rate of interest but favoured regulating the movement of specie. The author of *Policies* opposed regulating prices, as stated above. North did also – and made no distinction between domestic and foreign markets. Or did the author of *Considerations on the East-India Trade* (1701). They together with Gervaise and Whately were the only writers before Smith whom Viner said 'seem really to have been free traders'.[9] Actually North seems to have had fewer reservations, if he had any at all, than Smith had. Whately advocated bounties in the work from which his reputation as a free trader comes, *Principles of Trade* (1774), which he wrote with Benjamin Franklin. The work combines acute observations of the merit of free markets along with observations, acute or obtuse, of the circumstances in which markets should not be free.[10] In this, their tract was characteristic of those of the mercantilists and also resembled *The Wealth of Nations* which it preceded by only two years.

What the mercantilists anticipated about the market is noteworthy for its extent and also for being so little appreciated. To take note of it is to see they did (*pace* Heckscher[11]) 'penetrate the dark arcana of economic relationships'. The idea of demand and supply as schedules is in Berkeley's *Queries*; cross-elasticity is in Child; utility in Barbon; the usefulness of capital markets in Malynes and Misselden; the idea that consumption is or should be the object of all effort is in Defoe, Tucker, and Postlethwayt, just as it is in Smith and just as inconsistently.[12] Then there is the remarkable William Petty. He said (*pace* Viner[13]) that the interest on a sum at loan was (after adjusting for differences of risk) equal to the rent on the land which the sum could purchase and that the rent was equal to the value of output minus the other costs of producing it (which means rent is a component of cost and affects price rather than, as the classicists said, is determined by price). The cost of corn, and presumably of anything else, is the cost of an alternative product that could be produced with the same amount of labour. If that is not quite the idea of opportunity cost it is well on the way to it. Like the classicists, Petty had a labour theory of value, and his was that labour is the measure of value. He employed the idea of cross-elasticity of demand (a higher price of mutton will increase the demand for fish) and also used the idea of price-elasticity of demand (a 'picture-maker' who has more work than he has time for when his price is 5,1 will consider whether he can keep busy if he raises his price to 6,1). Like many mercantilists Petty thought England would be improved by an increase in its population because that would increase its capital stock and would also reduce the cost of government per person since the total cost would not rise as much as the population (economies of scale in government). He computed the cost and benefit of England's prohibiting the import of cattle from Ireland (cost exceeded the benefit) and did the same for measures to prevent the plague (benefit exceeded cost).[14]

This *catalogue raisonné* should include ideas he had which did not contribute to the progress of economics. He said that producing luxuries misused resources and consuming them made people less industrious. This was also said by other mercantilists including some who averred that consumption is the end of economic effort. Petty deplored 'wasteful spending' but (at least) did not contradict himself by saying consumption is the proper end of economic effort. Yet he was inconsistent in the way he proposed to eliminate wastefulness. The reason people make an economic effort, he said, is to improve their relative position, and this brings about wasteful spending (by those in the upper reaches of the distribution presumably). He went on to propose a tax that would reduce the income of the rich and their ability to spend wastefully. The proceeds were to pay for entertainment and magnificent shows provided by the government.

Wasteful he acknowledged them to be, but said they would place money in the hands of tradesmen. That in turn would increase employment, presumably by a multiplier effect.[15] Greater employment was a major objective of most of the writers throughout the period of mercantilism, and they wanted to increase the supply of labour as well as the demand for it.[16] Petty, like many others, also wanted the employment to be efficient. He would have allowed busy-work as an interim measure but as a permanent condition it would not improve England. Yet he did say the country would be better off if tillage replaced grazing because tillage used more labour.[17]

What the mercantilists said about employment appears most often among the ideas about foreign trade and money, and they are the ideas that have been the centre of historical inquiry. They are said to be mistaken, and the mistake is said to be what sets the mercantilists apart from later economists.

Most of them did say an excess of exports over imports is beneficial because it increases employment or the money stock or both. They were in fact mistaken if they meant a favourable balance of trade would increase employment in the long run (except if the surplus in the trade account was to be offset by a deficit in the capital account). But they were not so clearly mistaken, if mistaken at all, if they meant a favourable balance would increase employment in the short run. Whether or not it will depends on certain conditions, and if they are present employment will increase.

What the mercantilists said about employment has however received less attention than what they said about money, which most historians have concluded was at best confused and at worst altogether mistaken because they are supposed to have said money is wealth. Most of them did say an increase in the money stock is beneficial. But they did not, most of them, say an increase in the money stock is beneficial because it is an increase in the stock of physical capital as, say, an additional merchant vessel would be. To contend they did not know the difference between a financial and a real asset does them an injustice.

Many believed an increase in the amount of money in a nation would be favourable to 'trade', a term they used for what later was called aggregate spending, income, or output. The increase of course entailed an increase in employment. Just why more money meant more output was explained in two ways. One was that an increase in the quantity of money would lower the rate of interest which in turn would induce firms to increase their stock of goods. The other was simply that for each amount of trade and employment there was a certain amount of money needed and if there was to be more trade there must be more money.[18] (That is not much of an explanation, but it does not confuse money with wealth.)

The claim that an increase of the money stock means more trade and employment was not the only argument for increasing it. Money is a store of value (as the quantity theory states of course) and prudence directs a nation to acquire money for that purpose as well as for the purpose of improving trade (because it is a medium of exchange, another proposition of the quantity theory). As a store of value (the argument went) money gives a nation a command over foreign resources that can assist it in time of distress or emergency, the distress of a crop failure or the emergency of armed conflict. Money is 'the sinews of war', one reads again and again. Surely that means no more than that money is a store of value and does not mean money is wealth. Yet later economists have said it is either a specious claim or a confusion. Smith said that if a country needs goods or foreign mercenaries in wartime it can secure them by an export surplus (an acknowledgement incidentally that a favourable trade balance can be useful).[19] The mercantilist reply probably would have been that money is more liquid than a potential export surplus. Viner said a country could acquire money for war by domestic taxes.[20] Harry Johnson said that if the mercantilists did argue for more money on the ground that it would increase military power they nevertheless failed to see that when money came into the country it had to pass into the hands of the government.[21] They could not have been that simple-minded.

Yet suppose they were. Suppose too that they were simple-minded about foreign trade and believed, as alleged, that it yields no mutual advantage. Would that signify they anticipated nothing of later economics, hence that the classicists placed economics in an entirely different direction? Not at all. There would remain the large and important collection of ideas the mercantilists held about the operation of the market and which are described above. There would also remain the fact that the objective of their economic policy was similar to the objective of classical economic policy – to which the paper now turns.

II   The normative economics of mercantilism
Just what objective policy serves is a part of normative economics. The method of achieving the objective is positive economics. The mercantilists usually put them together because their arguments for change were supported by statements of how the economy operates. They said, for example, that the power of the country is greater the greater are its riches; that its riches will increase if employment increases, which it will do if the money stock is increased. Hence the money stock ought to be increased. What precedes 'hence' is a factual statement in the sense that it is refutable. What follows 'hence' is a statement of value because it implies power is desirable.

The relations between fact and value in mercantilist thinking were described in Part I. While it was mainly about positive propositions it had necessarily to describe the goals they were meant to support. What was not described there and is described here is the nature of the goals and their relation to political values. Simply put, it is about why the mercantilists believed the state should intervene in economic affairs.

When they argued for intervention their purpose was national improvement. When 'improvement' was specified it usually meant greater riches, and greater riches were to be sought because they brought greater power. But the mercantilists also spoke of other effects. Greater riches meant an improvement in the condition of the population or what today would be called an increase of per capita real income.[22] How the improvement was to be shared was alluded to, and what was said would not today be considered correct in all quarters. A belief common in the mercantilist period (and later as well) was that the poor are feckless, that as wages rise they work less, that a harsh environment makes them more industrious, that popular entertainments (cock fights, bear baiting, and cudgel playing) should be suppressed because they keep workers from their jobs.[23] But a few mercantilists differed. Defoe said high wages enabled the poor to spend more, hence were favourable to trade (an anticipation of early Keynesianism). Berkeley asked rhetorically, 'Whether as feed equally scattered produceth a goodly harvest, even so an equal distribution of wealth doth not cause a nation to flourish?' But he also said laziness should be dealt with severely.[24]

Prominent among the normative ideas of the mercantilists is the idea that state intervention can increase the efficiency of the economy, meaning intervention can increase output and contribute to national improvement. This places their argument for intervention on utilitarian grounds. Those are the grounds of classical economic policy as well and are the grounds on which most economists today place their arguments for or against intervention.

Moreover most economists are in agreement about the end of policy. It is efficiency in the sense of maximizing output. The circumstances in which it is maximized are described with subtlety and a certain elegance, something not even an admirer of the mercantilists could say they displayed. But they too said an increase in output is the purpose of policy. To be sure, they also said power was the purpose and they probably believed it was more important than efficiency. But the distinction does not make much of a difference. Economics at present either takes power for granted in analysing the conditions for efficiency or makes power a public good and so incorporates it in the analysis.

Utilitarianism is so common that it may be thought to be the only practical rule that could govern policy. But it is not. Policy can be based on a philosophy of rights; the objective then is the protection or fulfilment or the provision of rights to individuals. This is a fairly recent idea in the theory of economic policy but has long had a place in political philosophy. It has no place in what the mercantilists wrote about economic policy but there are traces of it in their remarks about political matters.[25]

Another idea that has no place in mercantilist economics is that an economy of free markets is a system which by its nature is harmonious and orderly. The idea is not itself a normative proposition but is an assertion of fact, namely, that the objective of efficiency, which is normative, can best be achieved by means of free exchange. It is said to make classical economics distinctly different from mercantilist doctrine.[26] But (as explained below) Smith made so many exceptions to the harmony of self-interest that he cannot be said to have justified his views of policy by it.

There is another normative foundation to be noticed – philosophic idealism. The mercantilists are said to have favoured the control of the economy by the state on the ground that individuals acting in their own interest could do harm to (and here things cloud over) the interest of the country or the interest of others or of the government or simply of 'the whole'.[27] In this interpretation the normative elements of mercantilism anticipate the idea of the comprehensive direction of the economy by the government for the purpose of achieving objectives and of attaining values that cannot be achieved by individuals acting in their own interest. Or, in plain language, mercantilism was the forerunner of communism and fascism. In a mild version of this interpretation, mercantilism anticipated the extreme forms of nationalism, those that authorize the government to direct investment, modify the composition of output by regulating consumption and other means, to engage in trade wars, to enlarge the public sector, and to have discretionary power over the choice of public goods. In the period between the world wars of this century, there was a welter of nationalism, and it was called a return to mercantilism.[28] In the last half of this century, mercantilism has been said to be the antecedent of industrial policy in the developed world and of the array of measures the rest of the world has employed to speed its development.

What must be acknowledged is that there is a resemblance between mercantilism and the belief that the government must have extensive authority over economic affairs. While a few of the mercantilists expressly said regulation should be the principle of policy, almost all of them made it the practice. They argued for this, that, or the other form of regulation, e.g., duties on imports, rebates on some, subsidies for some exports, taxes on others, the fixing of certain prices, specific taxes on particular goods, sumptuary control, workhouses, the disciplining of labour, usury laws, control of agricultural rents, and on and on. If all these measures had been advocated by all of the mercantilists, or by the best remembered of them, their doctrine then could be described correctly as a doctrine of comprehensive control of the economy by the state. But of course not all of the measures were advocated by any one of the mercantilists who, most of them, opposed some kinds of regulation while they favoured others. There was more diversity among the measures they advocated than there was among the measures advocated by the classical economists who were, however, by no means of one mind themselves.

This is not to deny that mercantilism had a transcendent purpose, just as idealist philosophy has, or that the purpose ran counter to the interest of particular people, again a feature of idealism. Moreover the transcendent mercantilist purpose was, more often than not, the enhancement of the state (another feature of idealism). What I would deny is that the mercantilists discovered this purpose in the nature of society or discerned it from something outside of themselves, as something decreed by history (Marx), or derived from myth (Croce and Sorel), or to be divined in God (Hegel).

III Classical economic policy

Classical policy differed from that of mercantilism in degree, not in kind or purpose. There was less regulation and more market in classical policy. But the market alone was certainly not to govern the economy.

Consider the actions of government of which Smith approved or which he would have it undertake because he believed the market could not do them properly, or do them at all, or should not do them even if it could. They constitute exceptions to the principle of free exchange. They do not repudiate it; they do limit its application. They have a place in *The Wealth of Nations* just as the simple system of natural liberty has. But they are less known.

The final book of *The Wealth of Nations* assigns three grand functions to government: the administration of justice, the defence of the nation and the provision of public works. Elsewhere in the work there are many more, some 25 or 30, depending on how one defines an exception. There are still more in his *Lectures on Jurisprudence*. Together they can be put into four groups.

The first and largest had to do with helping the individual as a buyer, a worker, or simply as a person in need of assistance of one kind or another. One kind was to be furnished by schools that would alleviate the adverse effects of the division of labour, such as cowardice and a want of the martial spirit. Another kind was to protect people from religious fanaticism (belief also?) by regulating the churches (in a way that would encourage indolence in the clergy of the established church and, among other denominations, promote the kind of competition that would make each of them ineffectual). As buyers, people were to be assisted by some goods being stamped with a mark of their quality (cloth and silver); by the price of food being fixed if production or distribution was monopolized; by placing an embargo on the export of grain in time of scarcity; by lowering the tax on beer and raising that on spirits in order to reduce the consumption of alcohol; and, for the same purpose, by imposing a tax on small alehouses. As workers, people were to be assisted by the state's requiring employers to pay wages in money instead of in goods (i.e., the truck system was to be prohibited). Smith approved of the state's acting on behalf of slaves in order that they be treated humanely and also to make them more productive.[29]

In the next largest group were measures to improve efficiency either by supplementing the market or restricting it. There were to be usury laws that would replace consumer loans with business loans; a prohibition of engrossing land in the colonies; the granting of temporary monopoly rights to firms that opened new markets in risky areas and for the same reason (to induce risk taking) the granting of patents and copyrights; and the authorization of monopoly in markets too small to support more than one seller.[30]

In the third group were the taxes Smith proposed on the value of land and on rent, and they were anything but neutral. He did, admittedly, take care that they should have as little 'inconveniency and oppression' as possible, but that did not mean making them consistent with a market allocation of resources and output. They were expressly meant to alter the way land was used, to encourage certain people to use it, and to influence the manner in which rents were paid. One of the taxes was meant, he said, to make the rich pay more than the poor for the support of government.

Taxes on rent, levied nominally on the landlord, were to be higher if the landlord required that his land be used in a specific way; they were to be higher if at the expiration of a lease he levied a 'fine' (immediate payment of a lump sum) instead of raising the rent; they were to be higher if the landlord did not occupy a part of his land; and they were to be higher if he wanted his rent in kind instead of money. Smith went on to consider a tax that would vary with the value of land (which itself would vary with the rent it yielded). He liked such a tax but acknowledged that it could dissuade a landlord from making improvements since they would increase his rent. To avoid this, Smith proposed what in effect was a tax incentive to investment. The value of the land was to be appraised before the improvement was made and was to be taxed at that value until the landlord had been fully indemnified for the improvement. Then there was the redistributive tax. It was on house rent, the rich and the poor paying the same percentage of their rent. But, Smith explained, because the rich spend a greater percentage of their income on rent than the poor spend, the rich would be made to contribute to the public expense a higher proportion of their revenue, in which 'there would not, perhaps, be anything very unreasonable'. Their magnificent houses, he said, serve to exhibit the 'luxuries and vanities of life'.[31] Also to be noticed is the sumptuary judgement which is consistent with his ideas about taxing alcohol.

The fourth group had to do with foreign trade. Some of the measures Smith advocated were restrictive even though he declared himself for the principle of free trade. The most important were to limit trade that could impair military power, and among the restrictive measures the most notable were the

Navigation Laws because, by common belief, they increased the size of the merchant marine and so contributed to defence. 'Defence', he said in a memorable statement, 'is of much more importance than opulence'. He approved (as Ricardo did later) of a duty on goods which when produced at home are subject to a domestic tax. Without it, there would be too little labour and capital used in the production of the domestically taxed good and too much in the production of other things.

Smith noted two other circumstances in which an import duty may be advantageous. One is that in which it may induce a foreign country to reduce its duty on British goods. The other is that in which the removal of a duty quickly and completely would leave large numbers without employment. What should be done, Smith advised, is to reduce the duty slowly, with reserve, and circumspection.

How significant are his qualifications to the practice of free trade? The question can be argued; and if it is, there are (I suggest) two aspects that merit attention. One is theoretical and the other practical or political.

On the theoretical side, one may ask if Smith got the theory wrong as the mercantilists are said to have done (and as some in fact did). Smith ridiculed their belief that an excess of exports over imports was favourable to a country.[32] Still, he did say a favourable balance was the means by which a country should acquire foreign goods and services in time of war. About a protective tariff, he said that while it might bring an industry into being sooner than a free market would it was nevertheless a waste of resources. Yet he did not oppose protection per se, certainly not the protection of one of Britain's venerable manufactures: the making of woollen goods. He advocated an export duty on raw wool in order to give British producers an advantage over their foreign competitors who also used British wool.[33]

The practical or political side of the question is whether Smith's policy for foreign trade was favourable or unfavourable to the eventual adoption of free trade as the policy of Great Britain. His views are said to have been a reason why Britain and France in the Eden Treaty of 1786 reduced barriers on each other's goods. What effect the Treaty could have had is unknown because it was set aside by the revolution in France. In 1820, the British government clearly set a course towards free trade. In the considerable debate that initiated the policy and accompanied its application, Smith was called on by the opponents of free trade as well as by its advocates. When the debate reached its finale between 1838 and 1845 in the controversy over the Corn Laws, the stated objective of the Anti-Corn Law League was 'Complete and immediate repeal – Not one shilling's duty, not one day's delay'. The free traders did not get that from Smith, which may or may not signify. What does signify is that none of his successors, the classical economists of the day, had an important part in the campaign.[34]

Foreign trade is not the only area of policy in which Smith is to be read with care. The public works which he made an obligation of government were presumably meant to increase the efficiency of the economy. Yet his argument for them is not consistent with the proposition he laid down and repeated any number of times: that the self-interest of owners of capital will direct them to place it in the most efficient uses. Not so for canals, roads, bridges, harbours, and the like. He does say, to be sure, that the profit from them is too small to interest the market in them. Yet he also says they will pay for themselves by the tolls levied for their use.[35]

Among all of the exceptions he made to free exchange he gave the least attention to what today are called public goods and goods having external effects. He did say people having a communicable disease should be quarantined, certainly a measure to control an externality; and he made the curious observation that banks should be prohibited from issuing notes in small denominations, admitting the prohibition was a violation of natural liberty but defending it as a safeguard analogous to firewalls.[36]

Finally, there is the invisible hand. It is said to be the beneficent power of the market or the equilibrating mechanism or the providential force of the natural order. Actually in the chapter where it is used, it simply means that self-interest at times contributes to national defence and helps to remedy a market failure.

Smith came by the utilitarianism of *The Wealth of Nations* understandably. It informed the philosophy of his friend David Hume who is also and mistakenly said to have been an extreme advocate of free markets, especially in foreign trade. Actually Hume did not oppose regulation to protect certain British goods (linen in Ireland and rum in the colonies). He said Henry VII was wise to have made loans to business firms at an interest rate below the market.[37] Then there is his interesting solution to the problem of choosing which public goods to produce. The sovereign decides, and his decision is not made after reading the utility schedules of his subjects, then computing alternative costs, followed by estimating a rate of return and comparing that with the highest alternative rate. Hume might have thought such scrupulous attention to the welfare of the people was praiseworthy, but he is not likely to have thought it worthwhile. This does not mean he was indifferent to the sum of welfare. It means he believed people in government were capable of knowing what that welfare was.

There is a similar idea in the theory of policy of John Stuart Mill who took utilitarianism (a word he invented) farthest in classical economics. He specified meticulously the conditions in which exceptions could properly be taken to the market and authority could be vested with the government. But having done that, he said, a few pages on, that there was 'scarcely anything really important' that should not be taken from the market if people of good intentions believe it should be or 'can be induced to believe' it should be. The next titan in the classical succession, Marshall, declared: 'So I cry, laissez faire; let the state be up and doing.'[38] Is there any reason to be surprised?

IV Coda

The argument of this chapter is simplicity itself. In mercantilist doctrine there are propositions that anticipate a substantial amount of later economics, including and especially classical economics. What they have in common is so important that the latter should be considered an extension of the former and the matter left at that.

Notes

1. John Deacon, *A Treatise Intitvuled*: *Nobody is my name Which beareth Eurie-bodies blame, Wherein is Largely laied forth the lawfull bounds of all buying and selling, according to the infallible line of the lawes of the Lord* (London, 1580), n.p.
2. *A Discourse of the Common Weal of This Realm of England*, ed. Elizabeth Lamond (Cambridge, 1893), pp. 59–60, 88, lxiii–lxiv, 122, 46. This edition attributes the work to John Hales. A later edition, edited by Mary Dewar (Charlottesville, 1969) attributes it to Thomas Smith.
3. Part III.
4. Anon., *Policies, etc.* in *Tudor Economic Documents*, ed. R.H. Tawney and Eileen Power (London, 1924), III, p. 317.
5. Ibid., III, p. 340.
6. Roger Bieston, *The bayte and snare of Fortune. Etc.* (London, 1558), Prologue; N. Hemming, or Niels Hemmington, to whom is attributed the second of two tracts bound together and entitled *A General Discourse Against the Damnable Sect of Usurers, etc. Whereunto is Annexed another Godlie Treatise concernying the Lawful Use of Ritches*, trans. Rogers (London, 1578), chap. I; Gerard Malynes, *Consuetudo vel Lex Mercatoria*: *or The Ancient Law Merchant* (London, 1622), pp. 4–5; Edward Misselden, *Free Trade, or the Meanes to Make Trade Florish* (London, 1622), pp. 55, 66; William Petty, *Economic Writings*, ed. Charles Henry Hull (Cambridge, 1899), I, p. 32; Nicholas Barbon, *A Discourse of Trade* [1690]. Reprint of Economic Tracts, ed. Jacob H. Hollander (Baltimore, 1905), p. 9; Josiah Child, *A New Discourse of Trade* (Glasgow, 1751), 5th ed., p. 81, (a revision of an edition published as early as 1690); Dudley North, *Discourses Upon Trade* [1691]. Reprint of Economic Tracts, ed. Jacob H. Hollander (Baltimore, 1907), pp. 27–8; [Charles Davenant,] *An Essay upon Ways and Means of Supplying the War* (London, 1695), pp. 17–18; [Daniel Defoe,] *The Complete English Tradesman, etc.* (London, 1732), II, pp. 79–80; [Josiah Tucker,] *A Brief Essay on ... Trade* (London, 1750), 2nd ed., pp. ix, 61–2; George Berkeley, *The Querist, or, Several Queries Proposed to the Consideration of the Public* (Glasgow, 1751), Q. 46, Q. 47; Malachy Postlethwayt, *The Universal Dictionary of Trade and Commerce* (London, 1759), 4th ed., cap. 'Europe'.
7. Malynes, *Consuetudo*, p. 67.
8. William R. Allen, 'The Position of Mercantilism and the Early Development of International Trade Theory' in *Events, Ideology and Economic Theory*, ed. Robert V. Eagly (Detroit, 1968), p. 72.
9. Viner, *Studies, etc.* p. 92.
10. William D. Grampp, 'The Political Economy of Poor Richard', *Journal of Political Economy*, **55**(2), April 1947, 133–4.
11. Eli F. Heckscher, *Mercantilism*, trans. Mendel Shapiro (London, 1935), II, p. 270.
12. Berkeley, *Querist*, Q. 24; Child, *New Discourses*, p. 54; Barbon, *Discourse*, p. 13; Malynes, *The Maintenance of Free Trade* (London, 1622), p. 98; Misselden, *Free Trade*, pp. 117–18; Defoe, *Complete English Tradesman*, I, pp. 318–19; Tucker, *Brief Essay*, p. i;

Postlethwayt, *Great Britain's Commercial Interest Explained and Improved* (London, 1759), 2nd ed., p. 395; Smith *Discourse*, p. 625.

13. Viner, *Studies, etc.*, p. 31.
14. Petty *Economic Writings*, I, p. 48; I, p. 211; I, p. 212; I, p. 59; I, 219; I, p. 35; I, p. 1. 'Some Observations made by Wm. Petty upon the trade of Irish Cattle', in *Papers Relating to Affairs of State in Ireland, etc.*, II, pp. 47–8, MS 1180, Trinity College Library, Dublin.
15. Petty, *Economic Writings*, I, pp. 32, 33.
16. William D. Grampp, 'The Liberal Elements in English Mercantilism', *Quarterly Journal of Economics*, **66**(4), (November 1952), pp. 468–71.
17. Petty, *Economic Writings*, I, pp. 60, 59.
18. See Grampp, 'The Liberal Elements in English Mercantilism', pp. 480–81.
19. Smith, *The Wealth of Nations* (New York, 1937), p. 409.
20. Viner, *Studies, etc.*, p. 25.
21. Harry G. Johnson, 'Mercantilism: Past, Present, and Future', *Manchester School*, **42**(1), (March 1974), pp. 1–11.
22. Henry Robinson, *Certaine Proposals in order to a new Modelling of the Lawes, etc.* (London, 1653), p. 13; Davenant, *Essay*, pp. 56–7; Defoe, *Complete English Tradesman*, I, pp. 318–19.
23. Defoe, *True Born Englishman* in *Essays and Studies by Members of the English Association*, collected by C.H. Herford (Oxford, 1913), IV; Petty, *Economic Writings*, I, pp. 274–5; Tucker, *Brief Essay*, pp. 53ff.
24. Davenant, *Essay*, pp. 103, 130; Berkeley, *Querist*, Q. 214, Q. 382.
25. Vide Grampp, *The Liberal Elements in English Mercantilism*, pp. 488–9.
26. Viner, *Studies, etc.*, p. 93.
27. Ibid., p. 94.
28. As good an example as any of this mistake is that made by the present writer himself in 'The Third Century of Mercantilism', *Southern Economic Journal*, April 1944, pp. 292–302.
29. Smith, *The Wealth of Nations*, pp. 737, 742–3, 122, 142, 507, 842, 804, 142, 553.
30. Ibid., pp. 339, 539, 712; Smith *Lectures on Jurisprudence* (Indianapolis, 1982), p. 86.
31. Smith, *The Wealth of Nations*, pp. 782–5, 794.
32. Ibid., p. 456.
33. Ibid., p. 618.
34. William D. Grampp, *The Manchester School of Economics* (Stanford, 1960), p. 98.
35. Smith, *The Wealth of Nations*, p. 767.
36. Ibid., p. 308.
37. David Hume, *The History of England, etc.* (London, 1923), **III**, p. 401.
38. John Stuart Mill, *Principles of Political Economy, etc.* (London, 1891), pp. 604, 627. Alfred Marshall, 'Economic Chivalry', *Memorials of Alfred Marshall*, ed. A.C. Pigou (New York, 1966), p. 336.

2 Stoicism in the *EPS*: the foundation of Adam Smith's moral philosophy

Paul A. Heise

In the Introduction to the Glasgow edition of *The Theory of Moral Sentiments* (*TMS*)[1] the editors, Raphael and Macfie, spend five pages discussing the 'influence of Stoic philosophy' on the *TMS*, stating that: 'Stoic philosophy is the primary influence on Smith's ethical thought. It also fundamentally affects his economic theory.' They then go on to note that 'Stoicism is given far more space than any other system', that 'Stoicism never lost its hold over Smith's mind', that 'Stoicism permeated his reflection over the whole range of ethics and social sciences', that 'Life according to nature was the basic tenet of Stoic ethics, and a Stoic idea of nature and the natural forms a major part of the philosophical foundations of TMS and WN alike', and finally that 'In the WN the Stoic concept of natural harmony appears especially in "the obvious and simple system of natural liberty"'.[2]

Those examining the life and work of Adam Smith often found this Stoic presence worth noting but seldom worth examining.[3] Nor is the Stoic presence or influence specifically denied.[4] This is changing as Smith is being put into a context broader than *The Wealth of Nations* (*WN*) and its specific use of prior economic sources.

This paper addresses the presence of Stoicism in Adam Smith's work. Section I is a review of some of the recent literature with reference to discussion of Smith and the Stoics. Section II looks at the direct references and the presence of Stoic thought in the *EPS*, as it forms the basis of his moral philosophy. Finally, Section III looks at some of the implications of a more Stoic reading of *TMS* in regard to one of the propensities, the partial spectator, and its application by Smith.

I Review of recent literature

Macfie's 1961 article 'The Scottish Tradition in Economic Thought' put Smith in the broader philosophical context of his century and suggested that there was something unique, unappreciated and truncated about the Scottish tradition and that it was worth studying, especially in regard to Adam Smith. The resulting mêlée is still a free-for-all with sociologists, historians and political scientists publishing in their own and economics journals.[5]

The history and political science train of inquiry includes a wide range of scholars and is best exemplified by the Cambridge University, King's College Research Centre project 'Political Economy and Society, 1750–1850' where the work of Hont and Ignatieff (1984) brings together the work of some of the most important scholars.

This work on Smith's politics intensified an emphasis on the appropriate language or 'voice' in which to read Adam Smith. This was firsts raised by Lindgren (1969) and then carried forward by, among others, Heilbroner (1982), Pocock (1985) and Evensky (1987). Smith is now also being subjected to a literary criticism that rejects, in a sense, the previous movement to context,[6] but significantly for this paper inserts a recognition of the Stoic elements. The first serious acceptance of a Stoic factor is in Waszek (1984), 'Two Concepts of Morality: Adam Smith's Ethics and its Stoic Origin'.[7] More recent and continuing is the work of Brown (1991), 'Signifying Voices: Reading the "Adam Smith Problem"' and (1992), 'The Dialogic Experience of Conscience: Adam Smith and the Voices of Stoicism'.[8]

The purpose of this paper is to argue in the traditional way the sources and presence of Stoicism in the philosophy and economics of Adam Smith.[9] I am also suggesting that Smith must be read in the language of the Stoics rather than that of the other candidates such as civic humanism, civil jurisprudence, etc.

II   Stoic thought in the *EPS*

This paper holds that Smith's published works – the *EPS*, *TMS*, and *WN* – present a cohesive model of human behaviour that he started early in life and continued to follow throughout all his work.[10] The sequence by which Smith builds his system of moral philosophy starts with a philosophical grounding in the *EPS*, moves on to a model of moral behaviour in *TMS*, which he then applies in *WN*. An often promised last book on jurisprudence was to complete the project.[11] However, over the years, few economists have read the totality of Smith's work and even careful scholars found problems in *TMS* or dismissed the *EPS*.[12]

In the model that Smith presents, both the physical base in *Senses* and the model of rational activity in *Languages* and *Astronomy* are almost completely Stoic. The ethics or moral sentiments of *TMS* are what Smith believed he was adding to that Stoic system to make individuals responsible for moral choices in regard to those whom they could know and affect.

Stoicism is not its popular caricature of detached passivism, but rather a full system of philosophy.[13] Stoicism is based on a physical universe, *physis*, which we know through the senses and of which mankind in its *logos* or rationality is the highest manifestation.[14] This is an animate cosmos of which we are part and to which we are responsible; but wherein everything has already been determined. Acceptance of nature, acting always 'in accord with nature', leads to the usually misunderstood tranquillity of the Wiseman. Individuals are the rational part of nature, and are 'virtuous' when they act rationally in conformity with nature. The Stoic seeks to be and the Wiseman is 'in accord with nature' and therefore has the tranquillity. The tranquillity is not the sought end. Those who are less than the perfect Wiseman are the Proficients who will always continue to strive. In the article by Waszek, this distinction between the Wiseman and the Proficient is seen to be repeated in Smith's distinction between 'virtue' and 'good offices'.

The fundamental Stoic propensity to one's own nature or self-interest, *oikeiosis*, and its concomitant directive to act 'according to nature' became not a call to quietism, *laissez-faire* or selfishness but a call to lead oneself and the community to their natural providential end. The individual, whatever his propensity to self-preservation or self-betterment, was called to be a part of the cosmos and to exercise his freedom in responsible membership in that cosmos, starting with himself but reaching out first to his family, community, and nation and then to the entire cosmos.

Smith rejected the Stoic animate nature of the universe and the Stoic universalism. In practical terms, Smith rejected that part of Stoicism which made God the impartial spectator.[15] He ignored the determinism, accepted virtually everything else, and felt that he added to Stoicism when he made the impartial spectator human. It can be argued [16] that this change constitutes a rejection of Stoicism but it is the position of this paper that Smith intended to add another dimension to or complete the Stoic model rather than reject it. A careful reading of Part VI of T*MS* as Smith's 'death song' shows that he was in 1789 more Stoic than ever.

The *EPS* includes: *Astronomy*, *Ancient Logics*, *Ancient Physics*, *External Senses*, *Imitative Arts*, *English and Italian Verses*, and *Languages*.[17] When these essays are taken in a philosophically logical sequence, the progression is from physics to logic to metaphysics and then ethics. In the essays that were to be the first part of Smith's 'great work', he presents a Stoic model of human behaviour – an empirical world where a benevolent deity put into mankind certain propensities that, when mankind is being rational or in accord with nature, lead to the propagation and prosperity of mankind and the enhancement of the cosmos. The Stoics and Adam Smith accept a human nature of natural propensities such as that to self, that is, the self-interest or self-betterment of Smith is the *oikeiosis* of the Stoics. This is the Stoic system and Smith's system, but only so long as he is dealing with the propensities where we are 'conducted by nature'. Smith actually identifies two sets of propensities: those which are from nature and those based on the needs of the faculties of speech and reason. While the essays are the place where Smith first posits the nature of his universe and its bundle of propensities that explain human behaviour, it is not until *WN* that he specifically states that there are these two kind of propensities: those that are 'original principles in human nature' and those that are 'the necessary consequence of the faculties of reason and speech'.[18]

This division repeats a breakdown that appears in *Languages* where impulses are 'partly compelled by necessity and partly conducted by nature', which indicates that Smith had and was using the concept much earlier than in *WN*.[19] The propensities from nature always accomplish their end of having beneficial effects for the system. But this second set of propensities, which arise because Smith goes beyond the Stoics, can have effects that are not guided by any benevolent invisible hand. On the contrary, in certain 'natural' situations, they have serious entropic effects for the system. Smith wants to explain more than the Stoics and go beyond their determinism. When he does, he encounters certain problems that appear first in the essays.

In *External Senses* and *Ancient Physics* Smith makes his most basic assumption in the acceptance of a physical or corporeal universe of which man is a coherent part. The actual content of these two essays is Stoic: the world is an organic whole, with a benevolent intelligence seeking its preservation and prosperity; a physical world of matter, with no incorporeal or metaphysical existences; and a world known only through the senses whose perception is always changing and, therefore, an inconstant basis on which to make judgements. As in most instances where Smith does not state a direct comparison of his own position with the Stoics, he merely presents as his own a physical or moral world that is consistent in virtually every respect with the Stoic world.

Here Smith makes a deistic/Stoic statement of his belief in an organic whole that takes care of its own prosperity but does not extend any regard to the prosperity or conservation of the individual.[20] Both Smith and the Stoics project a design in the universe, a benevolent guardian, a teleology of conservation and prosperity, and a non-malignant neglect of the individual. These essays are more a comment on the physics of the material world than on the physiology or psychology of the way that we perceive it. Sensations are, in fact, not to be trusted; they require, as the Stoics point out, a test of reason and an act of assent. Smith repeatedly points out that they are by their nature fleeting: 'no man ever saw, or heard, or touched the same sensible object twice'.[21] This impermanence sends us necessarily from the perception of the individual to the study of human nature.[22] This is of fundamental importance: it means that the individual cannot be, and is not, in Smith's system, the actor of interest. Human nature is the actor. It is the perfection and happiness of human nature that is the great end in both the Stoic and Smithian systems.[23]

The principal vehicle by which Adam Smith presented his metaphysics was the essay 'Considerations Concerning the First Formation of Languages'.[24]

This essay is not a philological study but, rather, an attempt to establish a modern logic and metaphysics on his understanding of the Stoic base he had received. Language,[25] quite aside from metaphysics, is central to Smith's and the Stoics' system of understanding the world and human nature. *Languages* establishes the basic human intellectual actions that lead to the classification and analysis of received sense perceptions.

The essay *Languages* begins with two savages trying to communicate, but Smith immediately departs from this to concentrate on the development of his logic and metaphysics as the explanation of their progress in language. Smith takes the savages through the recognition of qualities and relationships and points out their need to develop language to express adjectives, which 'required more metaphysics than we are apt to be aware of'[26] and prepositions, where a relation reflects a 'more metaphysical object than a quality'. The work continues to build a metaphysics covering colour, time, place, and even number, 'one of the most abstract and metaphysical ideas, which the mind of man is capable of forming'.[27] It also discusses the ordering of data, such as: the presentation of memory and association of memory to begin classification;[28] the progressively metaphysical nature of the development of language;[29] the metaphysical uniqueness of the individual;[30] and the demonstration of how the invisible hand in natural propensity systems permits the breakdown of man-made systems such as language.[31]

However, an important part of the model in *Languages* is the second part of the title: *The Different Genius of Original and Compounded Languages.*[32] The problem is that the language propensities – a love of analogy and a love of similarity of sound – that are 'compelled by necessity' produce when languages are compounded an important aspect of Smith's system; one that is noted with concern and puzzlement: the problem of system breakdown. There is an entropy that flows from the natural operation of the system.[33] Peoples with different languages *naturally* mix and the resulting entropy *naturally* destroys the beauty, conciseness, and flexibility of language.[34] These early essays build a logical humanity with the faculties of speech and reason, but they are passive even in their logic. The next step is to go from classification and passive recognition to impose order, sequence, and causation on the world around us. Smith does this in *Astronomy*.

The essay on the 'Principles which Lead and Direct Philosophical Enquiries', usually referred to as *Astronomy*, takes the structure of ideas and patterns repeated in time and adds chains of cause and effect. This is the full use of rationality and the sense in which the Stoics use reason. The actor in *Astronomy* can determine what is 'in accord with nature'. In *Astronomy*, Smith presents the 'Principles which Lead and Direct Philosophical Enquiries' as those which lead all rational inquiry or thought. It is in this essay that Smith completes the model of behaviour that corresponds to the Stoic model.

The content of *Astronomy* is usually treated as the presentation of a theory of knowledge or inquiry, a history of philosophy and science, or a history of astronomy.[35] It is all of these. But it is also the positing of the model for a rational animal, or for human nature. In this essay, Smith explains how mankind can know the data well enough to make rational choices about what is or is not in conformity with nature. Here Smith gives us his psychological 'machine' in regard to propensities, the importance of the imagination in moving us to action, and the tranquillity that comes with being in accord with nature, whether or not one has security.[36]

This essay provides the basic structure of the model that Smith assumes throughout the rest of his work. The early essays provided a model of animal behaviour and propensities to survival. Now, mankind will be active and make choices, but these choices are not yet moral. Smith is proposing a model for scientific or philosophical action or any intellectual act that needs propensities beyond the orientations of the Stoics. Here Smith finds them in wonder and surprise but he also ties it all to the Stoics in that the action arises from a need for tranquillity, a need to ease the tumult of the imagination.

Finally, we turn to the phrase 'invisible hand' which first arises in *Astronomy*.[37] Smith assigns the invisible hand expressly to a deity, in this case Jupiter. Smith accuses the pre-scientific community of not understanding and therefore not assigning 'the invisible hand of Jupiter' to the regular events of nature and the hand of man to irregular events. He notes that men 'never act but to ... alter natural events'.[38] Smith here very clearly and very early makes God's actions support nature while man's actions are meant to alter nature. The invisible hand, Smith here suggests, will not be allowed its purpose.[39]

The model of human behaviour in *TMS* completes the system. The *TMS* model with the impartial spectator judging the actions of ourselves and others in regard to their propriety is fairly well known. Also well known is the critique of Stoicism in Part VII, where Smith says that 'The plan and system which Nature has sketched out for our conduct seems to be altogether different from that of the Stoical philosophy'.[40] This dismissal rests on the Stoic idea that God is the impartial spectator.[41]

The problem, Smith says, is that the Stoic, in attempting to make God his impartial spectator, removed himself from the level of human understanding. From the perspective of a transcendent God, nothing man does has much relevance. Smith believed this was the point at which the Stoic system failed and the point at which he made a proper remedy with the human impartial spectator. But Smith does not condemn the Stoic attempt:

> Such was the philosophy of the Stoics. ...to the greater part of whose precepts there can be no other objection, except that honourable one, that they teach us to aim at a perfection altogether beyond the reach of human nature. (*TMS*, ed. 2–5, I.iii.3, p. 60)

In the sixth edition of *TMS*, Smith became even more Stoic when he reversed his position to state that such resignation is not impossible: 'Nor does this magnanimous resignation to the will of the great Director of the universe seem in any respect beyond the reach of human nature.'[42]

TMS presents 'a proper remedy and correction. The real or even imaginary presence of the impartial spectator'.[43] Smith seeks propriety in conformity with feelings that are generated from a habitual sympathy, i.e., that affection which we feel from the regular interaction with those, like family, friends and countrymen, whom we know, affect and, therefore, care about. Prudence, in Smith's meaning of self-interest, is bounded by the obligations of kinship that flow from sympathy for those we know and by benevolence and justice in regard to those for whom we have no natural affection.[44]

Smith's Stoicism is as pervasive and long-lasting as described by Raphael and Macfie with consequences that are profound for the understanding of the work of Smith and its application of concepts like the invisible hand and system of natural liberty to modern society. But it is now appropriate to show an application of this Stoic model and discover why it matters.

III Implications

In a system of natural liberty, nature will take care of the human race through that system of natural propensities which have been installed in humanity, so that human beings will act accordingly, whether or not they recognize the purpose. However, human nature also motivates the individual to act on the basis of those propensities that result from the faculties of speech and reason, and these, while necessary to nature's purpose, are the cause of all the troubles of mankind. Smith actually lists many such propensities but he is most specific about one that is especially important and not well known – the partial spectator.[45] This is merely one example of the operation of this system of human propensities.

Smith regularly refers to the 'supposed' impartial spectator because the spectator cannot be counted on to be impartial when, as in Smith's system, the spectator is human. A 'partial' spectator panders to the group and re-inforces selfish motives that sympathy would normally curtail, producing thereby the problems of faction. The partial spectator is associated with the fact that those around us share the benefits of a specific outcome, and looking to the benefits, those spectators who share the benefits reinforce our partiality to ourselves rather than moderate it.

Applications of the principle of the partial spectator extend from the seem-ingly trivial, like 'clubs and cabals' where they 'celebrate the talents and virtues of one another' and put down anyone who might come into competi-tion with them,[46] to the 'conduct of one independent nation towards another' where 'neutral nations are the only indifferent and impartial spectator.'[47]

'The indulgent and partial spectator is at hand: while the indifferent and impartial one is at a great distance.'[48] The problem of the nation state is important because that is where a state of natural liberty truly exists and where the resultant insecurity gives rise to every manner of distrust.[49]

Smith says that human nature is such that the gains to the nation, the largest comprehensible unit we can affect, come best in the presence of a 'system of natural liberty'. But he also says at the same time that such a system has built-in and necessary propensities that not only harm the individual but destroy the system itself, unless the individuals take care of each other and protect themselves through group action. These entropic destabilizing problems are natural to the system, for instance, with regard to language[50] and to the division of labour.[51] But the partial spectator's motivations to act are also contrary to nature and morally responsive to the needs of family, friends and nation.

System stability is important to Smith's system but God and man have separate tasks to make the system work. Smith clearly specifies and differentiates the separate roles of God and man.[52] The rather limited role of God is spelled out by Smith, when he assigns nature her role and man his. The evil that might befall the individual is not one of God's concerns; nor is the system one of man's.[53] Individual concerns – parity in material prosperity, civic or commercial freedom, or individual opportunity – are not part of God's plan for harmony and are not delivered by the invisible hand in the system of natural liberty. The individual is not God's concern, but he is man's concern.

The role of man is to take care of himself, his family, his friends and his nation, a role Smith clearly delineates for mankind. At times man as a self-interested individual is led and even forced to the irrational by nature and its propensities. The role of man as part of the system is such that many of his 'impotent endeavours' are at times so counter-productive to the individuals concerned as to 'shock all his natural sentiments'. The passages warning of these problems are not generally well known, probably because they are so contrary to the reigning perception of Smith:

> The natural course of things cannot be entirely controlled by the impotent endeavours of man: the current is too rapid and too strong for him to stop it; and though the rules which direct it appear to have been established for the wisest and best purposes, they sometimes produce effects which shock all his natural sentiments. That a great combination of men should prevail over a small one; ... seems to be a rule not only necessary and unavoidable in itself, but even useful and proper for rousing the industry and attention of mankind. Yet, when in consequences of this rule, violence and artifice prevail over sincerity and justice, what indignation does it not excite in the breast of every human spectator. (*TMS*, III.5.10, p. 168)

God assigned man the moral responsibility not only to act where he has competence and understanding, but to act virtuously, that is, to act to thwart or repair the damage caused by God's protection of the system.

> Thus man is by Nature directed to correct, in some measure, that distribution of things which she herself would otherwise have made. The rules which for this purpose she prompts him to follow, are different from those which she herself observes. (*TMS*, III.5.9, p. 168)

In the world of human behaviour or moral sentiments that Smith describes the invisible hand of God may indeed guide the system to a providential end but man is assigned responsibility to undo nature and the systemic entropic effects of a system of natural liberty. Smith would have us accept nature and its outcomes but only after doing all we can to moderate its effects.[54] Unlike the Stoics, personal responsibility for action is morally prior to that acceptance.

In the end, Smith goes beyond Stoic determinism and accepts that humanity taking care of its responsibilities is also picking up after God's seeming injustice, deception and unfairness. Man taking care of himself, his family, friends and country is the subject of the *Wealth of Nations*; picking up after God, where the self is not immediately concerned, was to be the subject of the work on jurisprudence.

Notes

1. The standard abbreviations from the Glasgow edition of the *Works and Correspondence and of Adam Smith* will be used throughout this paper.
2. *TMS*, Introduction, pp. 5–10.
3. Virtually everyone writing in general about Smith mentions the Stoics. These include: Marshall (1920 [1982], pp. 608–9), Schumpeter, 1954, pp. 65–6), Grampp (1965, pp. 1–47), Viner (1927, pp. 202–6), Hont and Ignatieff (1984, p. 10), and Pocock (1984, pp. 237 and 249). But no one until very recently followed up beyond the five pages in Raphael and Macfie (1976).
4. Two recent authors deny the Stoic influence. Lindgren (1973) claims there is an attempt to interpret *TMS* in Stoic terms which effort has experienced 'disappointment at not being able to confirm the hypothesis' (p. 35). The sources he cites: Hasbach (1891, pp. 129–47), Viner (1927, pp. 202–6), Gray (1933, p. 125), and Grampp (1965) do not bear him out. Dickey (1986, p. 592), the second demurrer, merely dismisses the Raphael and Macfie statement with 'I take exception to this view' that Smith's work 'from 1759 to 1790 was consistently oriented by Stoic principles'.
5. Another basis for an intensification of interest in every aspect of Adam Smith was laid in the accessibility provided by the Glasgow edition of the *Works and Correspondence of Adam Smith* and the Liberty Classic reissue. Everyone now has immediately at hand the *EPS*, the *TMS*, his lectures (*LJ(A)*, *LJ(B)* and rhetoric) and his Correspondence, as well as the *WN*.
6. Brown (1991, p. 189), an economist, best specifies the deconstructive nature of her approach: 'By concentrating on the literariness of Smith's texts, and by exploring the stylistic and moral divergence between TMS and WN, this article will demonstrate the textual identity of each of these works in a way that is not simply reducible to the issue of

authorial coherence or consistency.' Brown eschews (p. 187) 'intellectual biography' or trying to understand in terms of 'Smith's travels in France, Smith's meeting with the Physiocrats, or the mental capacities of an aging man'.

7. Waszek relates Smith's ethics directly to Stoic ethics and makes a Smith-like promise: 'The author hopes to follow up the present article with accounts of Hutcheson's indebtedness to the Stoic *sensus communis* and Hume's criticism of the Stoics.' I have not as yet found any record of such publications.

8. Brown has also published a book: *Commerce and Conscience: Reading Adam Smith's Discourse* (London: Routledge, 1994).

9. This paper is taken in part from my dissertation *Adam Smith and the Stoics* (UMI Microfilm, 1991).

10. Smith acknowledged his early purpose of creating a great work (Corres., p. 168). Bonar noted and others agree, 'Adam Smith undoubtedly started with the purpose of giving the world a complete social philosophy' (Bonar, 1893 [1967], p. 149).

11. The last paragraph of the 1759 edition of *TMS* (p. 342) promises both the *WN* and 'another discourse' on 'law and government'. There is a final reminder of this promise in the advertisement to the 6th edition of *TMS* in 1790, p. 4.

12. Dugald Stewart rejected *TMS* as early as 1793: 'I must confess, that [*TMS*] does not coincide with my notions concerning the foundation of morals' (*EPS*, p. 290). More recently, Edwin Cannan, editor's Introduction (1896, pp. xi–xxxiv) to Adam Smith, *Lectures on Justice, Police, Revenue and Arms* (Oxford: Clarendon Press, p. xiv), made light of the essays, and Wightman, the Glasgow edition editor of *EPS*, disparages (his word) these essays (*EPS*, pp. 1–27).

13. Stocism is not widely recognized as an historical influence or school of significance nor as being worthy of study despite the fact that it was the ruling paradigm of the ancient world for over 400 years. Shaw, for example, writes: '(T)oday there is no major philosophical system from antiquity that commands less interest or is considered intrinsically less penetrating as an intellectual adventure than Stoicism.' Shaw (1984), p. 18. Stoicism is today neglected, and even rejected, perhaps because its image is taken to be, as Grampp puts it, 'austere, unworldly, passive, and a little sour' Grampp (1965, p. 4.).

14. The principal modern sources on the Stoics, in English, are: Sandbach (1975) and Rist (1969). Rist also edited a volume of essays (1978). An earlier text that summarizes the state of the older scholarship is Bevan (1913).

    In German the works of M. Pohlenz, especially *Stoa und Stoiker* (Zurich, 1950) and *Die Stoa: Geschichte einer geistigen Bewegung* (Göttingen, 1948) are the standard sources.

    In the original Greek and Latin, the collection of references and fragments that still exist are gathered in H. von Arnim, *Stoicorum Veterum Fragmenta* (*SVF*), Reprint, Stuttgart 1964.

15. *TMS*, VII.ii.i.40, p. 290.

16. Brown (1992, p. 244) says that 'in substituting imagination for reason as the prime moral mover, the TMS privileged nature over reason and, ultimately, rejected Stoicism itself'. Brown has previously associated reason in this case with the divine being. Actually, in the Stoic system nature and reason are not separable. Smith privileged sentiments over reason.

17. The full titles, which are not without significance, are: 'The Principles which lead and direct Philosophical Enquiries: illustrated by the History of Astronomy', and separately, by the 'History of Ancient Physics' and by the 'History of Ancient Logics and Metaphysics'; 'Of the External Senses', 'Of the Nature of that Imitation which takes place in what are called The Imitative Arts' and 'Of the Affinity between certain English and Italian Verses'; and finally 'Considerations concerning the First Formation of Languages', which was printed by Smith with the *TMS* and the only one of these essays to be published in his lifetime (*Works and Correspondence of Adam Smith*, Vols III and IV).

18. 'Whether this propensity (to barter) be one of those original principles in human nature, of which no further account can be given; or whether, as seems more probable, it be the necessary consequence of the faculties of reason and speech', *WN*, I.ii.2, p. 25.

19. *Languages*, 30, p. 218.

20. 'The idea of an universal mind, of a God of all, who originally formed the whole, and who governs the whole by general laws, directed to the conservation and prosperity of the whole, without regard to that of any private individual, was a notion to which they (the savages) were utterly strangers.' *Ancient Physics*, 9, p. 113.
21. *Ancient Logic*, p. 120; and *External Senses*, 59, p. 155.
22. 'Our sensations, therefore, never properly exist or endure one moment; but, in the very instant of their generation, perish and are annihilated for ever. ... Things of so fleeting a nature can never be the objects of science, or of any steady or permanent judgment. But humanity, or human nature, is always existent, is always the same, is never generated, and is never corrupted. This, therefore, is the object of science, reason, and understanding.' *Ancient Logic*, p. 121.
23. *TMS*, III.5.9, p. 165.
24. This is the only one of these essays that was published in Smith's lifetime. It first appeared anonymously in *The Philological Miscellany* in May 1761, but was appended to the 3rd (1767) and later editions of *TMS*.
25. See Michael Frede, 'Principles of Stoic Grammar' and Andreas Graeser, 'The Stoic Theory of Meaning' in Rist (1978).
26. *Languages*, 7, p. 207.
27. *Languages*, 22, p. 214.
28. *Languages*, 1, p. 204.
29. *Languages*, 12, pp. 209–10.
30. *Languages*, 32, p. 219.
31. *Languages*, 42–3, p. 224.
32. Languages are 'compounded' when two peoples are mixed and each has to learn to communicate in a non-native language. The natural process is for the language to lose inflection, become simpler, and in the process become less efficient.
33. Heilbroner (1975).
34. *Languages*, 33 et seq., pp. 220–26.
35. Lindgren (1969), has probably the best overall view of *Astronomy* as a theory of inquiry. Lindgren suggests that language as an 'imitative art' is the prototype of the analysis that Smith uses in all other areas.
36. The content of this essay is in *Astronomy*, Parts I–III, pp. 33–53 and pp. 104–5. It should also be noted that while Smith presents the Stoic system of astronomy, he considered it worthless. *Astronomy*, IV.15, pp. 63–4.
37. The standard on this use of the 'invisible hand' is Macfie (1971). This work seems to think that Smith used the phrase differently here than in the other two instances in *TMS* and *WN*. Smith's use is the same in all three places: Jupiter in this case, or nature in the other two instances, act to ensure that 'fire burns and water refreshes' and all other natural things come to pass. This is in contrast to the savages who assign a nature-disrupting role to their gods.
38. *Astronomy*, III.2, p. 49.
39. Smith makes this point even more clearly in Part IV of *TMS*. See below.
40. *TMS*, VII.ii.1.43, p. 292.
41. 'The Stoical wise man endeavoured to enter into the views of the great Superintendent of the universe, and to see things in the same light in which that divine Being beheld them. But, to the great Superintendent of the universe, all the different events which the course of his providence may bring forth, what to us appear the smallest and the greatest, the bursting of a bubble, as Mr. Pope says, and that of a world, for example, were perfectly equal...', *TMS*, VII.ii.i.40, p. 290.
42. *TMS*, VI.ii.3.3–4, p. 235. He may have thought at the end of his life that David Hume or he himself had reached that exalted state.
43. *TMS*, VII.ii.1, p. 43.
44. *TMS*, VI. concl.3, pp. 262–4.
45. The partial spectator was noted by Coase (1976), p. 535; and by Lamb (1974), who recognizes the full implication but accepts Smith's reliance on the need and power of self-command to overcome this partiality at the level of the individual.

46. *TMS*, VI.i.7, p. 213.
47. *TMS*, III.42, p. 154.
48. *TMS*, III.3.41, p. 154.
49. *TMS*, VI.ii.2.4, p. 229.
50. *Languages*, 33 et seq., pp. 220–26.
51. '[M]an whose whole life is spent in performing a few simple operations, ... generally becomes as stupid and ignorant as it is possible for a human creature to become. ... Of the great and extensive interests of his country, he is altogether incapable of judging; and unless very particular pains have been taken to render him otherwise, he is equally incapable of defending his country in war.' *WN*, V.i.f.50, p. 782.
52. Evensky (1987), with his two voices of the moral philosopher and the social critic, recognizes the same dichotomy in Smith as is used here. Evensky, however, puts the phenomenon more in the presentation by Smith than in the analytical model: Smith 'presents two analyses, each built on a different set of premises' (p. 448). He also concludes that this is a means to solving the consistency problem.
53. 'The administration of the great system of the universe, however, the care of the universal happiness of all rational and sensible beings, is the business of God and not of man.' *TMS*, VI.ii.3.5, p. 236.
54. But mankind in the end is to submit in a perfectly Stoic fashion: 'By this admiration of success we are taught to submit more easily to those superiors, whom the course of human affairs may assign to us; to regard with reverence, and sometimes even with a sort of respectful affection, that fortunate violence which we are no longer capable of resisting; ...not only the violence of such splendid characters as those of Caesar or Alexander, but often that of the most brutal and savage barbarians, of an Attila, a Genghis, or a Tamerlane.' (*TMS*, VI.iii.30, p. 253)

References

Documentation

Adam Smith: The Glasgow edition of the *Works and Correspondence of Adam Smith*, Liberty Classics edition. Indianapolis: Liberty Press, 1987.

Vol. I.   *The Theory of Moral Sentiments* (1759), edited by A.L. Macfie and D.D. Raphael.
Vol. II.   *An Inquiry into the Nature and Causes of the Wealth of Nations* (1776), Edited by R.H. Campbell and A.S. Skinner.
Vol. III. *Essays on Philosophical Subjects* (published posthumously, 1795), edited by W.P.D. Wightman.
           History of Astronomy
           History of Ancient Physics
           History of Ancient Logics and Metaphysics
           Of the External Senses.

Other Sources

Ahmad, Syed (1990), 'Adam Smith's four invisible hands', *History of Political Economy*, **22**(1), pp. 137–44.
Bevan, Edwyn (1913), *Stoics and Skeptics*, Oxford: Clarendon Press.
Bitterman, H.J. (1940), 'Adam Smith's Empiricism and the Law of Nature, Parts I–II', *Journal of Political Economy*, **48**(4), August, pp. 487–520; October, pp. 703–34. Page references are to the reprint from Wood, below.
Bonar, James (1893 [1967]), *Philosophy and Political Economy in Some of their Historical Relations*, New York: Allen and Unwin.
Brown, Vivienne (1991), 'Signifying Voices: Reading the "Adam Smith Problem"', *Economics and Philosophy*, **7**, pp. 187–220.
Brown, Vivienne (1992), 'The Dialogic Experience of Conscience: Adam Smith and the Voices of Stoicism', *Eighteenth Century Studies*, **26**(2), Winter, 233–59.

Brown, Vivienne (1994), *Adam Smith's Discourse: Canonicity, Commerce and Conscience*, New York: Routledge.

Campbell, R.H. and A.S. Skinner (1982), *Adam Smith*, New York: St Martin's Press.

Coase, R.H. (1976), 'Adam Smith's View of Man', *The Journal of Law and Economics*, **19**, pp. 529–46.

Dickey, Laurence (1986), 'Historicizing the "Adam Smith Problem": Conceptual, Historiographical, and Textual Issues', *The Journal of Modern History*, **58**(3), pp. 579–609.

Evensky, Jerry (1987), 'The two voices of Adam Smith: moral Philosopher and social critic', *History of Political Economy*, **19**(3), 447–68.

Evensky, Jerry (1989), 'The Evolution of Adam Smith's Views on Political Economy', *History of Political Economy*, **21**(1), pp. 123–45.

Evensky, Jerry (1993), 'Retrospectives: Ethics and the Invisible Hand', *Journal of Economic Perspectives*, **7**(2) Spring, pp. 197–205.

Forbes, Duncan (1975), 'Sceptical Whiggism, Commerce, and Liberty', in Andrew Skinner and Thomas Wilson, eds, *Essays on Adam Smith*, Oxford: Clarendon Press.

Grampp, Wm (1965), *Economic Liberalism*, 2 vols, New York: Random House.

Gray, Alexander (1933), *The Development of Economic Doctrine*, New York: Wiley.

Hasbach, Wilhelm (1891), *Untersuchungen über Adam Smith und die Entwicklung der Politischen Ökonomie*, Leipzig: Duncker & Humblot.

Heilbroner, Robert L. (1975), 'The Paradox of Progress: Decline and Decay in *The Wealth of Nations*', in Andrew Skinner and Thomas Wilson, eds, *Essays on Adam Smith*, Oxford: Clarendon Press.

Heilbroner, Robert L. (1982), 'The Socialization of the Individual in Adam Smith', *History of Political Economy*, **14**(3), pp. 427–39.

Hont, Istvan and Michael Ignatieff, eds (1984), *Wealth and Virtue: The Shaping of Political Economy in the Scottish Enlightenment*, Cambridge: Cambridge University Press.

Inwood, Brad (1985), *Ethics and Human Action in Early Stoicism*, New York: Oxford University Press.

Lamb, Robert B. (1974), 'Adam Smith's System: Sympathy not Self-Interest', *Journal of the History of Ideas*, **35**, pp. 671–82.

Land, Stephen K. (1977), 'Adam Smith's "Considerations concerning the First Formation of Languages"', *Journal of the History of Ideas*, **38**, pp. 677–90.

Lindgren, Ralph J. (1969), 'Adam Smith's Theory of Inquiry', *Journal of Political Economy*, **77**, pp. 897–915.

Lindgren, Ralph J. (1973), *The Social Philosophy of Adam Smith*, The Hague: Martinus Nijhoff.

Macfie, A.L. (1961), 'The Scottish Tradition in Economic Thought', *Scottish Journal of Political Economy*, **8**, pp. 81–103.

Macfie, A.L. (1967), *The Individual in Society*. London: Allen and Unwin.

Macfie, A.L. (1971), 'The Invisible Hand of Jupiter', *History of Political Economy*, **32**, pp. 595–9.

Marshall, Alfred (1920 [1982]), *Principles of Economics*, 8th Edn, Philadelphia: Porcupine Press.

Oestreich, Gerhard (1982 [1969]), *Neo-Stoicism and the Early Modern State*, Cambridge: Cambridge University Press.

Pocock, J.G.A. (1984), 'Cambridge paradigms and Scotch philosophers: a study of the relationship between the civic humanist and the civil jurisprudential interpretation of eighteenth century social thought', in Istvan Hont and Michael Ignatieff, eds (1984), *Wealth and Virtue: The Shaping of Political Economy in the Scottish Enlightenment*, Cambridge: Cambridge University Press.

Pocock, J.G.A. (1985), *Virtue, commerce, and history: essays on political thought and history, chiefly in the eighteenth century*, Cambridge: Cambridge University Press.

Raphael, D.D. (1975), 'The Impartial Spectator', in Andrew Skinner and Thomas Wilson, eds, *Essays on Adam Smith*, Oxford: Clarendon Press.

Raphael, D.D. and A.L. Macfie (1976), 'Introduction' to Adam Smith (1759 [1982]), *The Theory of Moral Sentiments*, Indianapolis: Liberty Classics.

Rist, J.M. (1969), *Stoic Philosophy*, New York: Cambridge University Press.

Rist, J.M. ed. (1978), *The Stoics*, Berkeley: University of California Press.

Rosenberg, Nathan (1990), 'Adam Smith and the stock of moral capital', *History of Political Economy*, **22**(1), pp. 1–17.

Rothschild, Emma (1992), 'Adam Smith and conservative economics', *Economics History Review*, **XLV**(1), pp. 74–96.

Sandbach, F.H. (1975), *The Stoics*, New York: Norton.

Schumpeter, Joseph A. (1954), *History of Economic Analysis*, New York: Oxford University Press.

Shaw, Brent D. (1984), 'The Divine Economy: Stoicism as Ideology', *Latomus*, **44**(1), pp. 16–54.

Skinner, Andrew S. (1976), 'Adam Smith: the Development of a System', *Scottish Journal of Political Economy*, **23**(2), 111–32.

Skinner, Andrew S. (1988), 'Adam Smith', *The New Palgrave*, pp. 357–74.

Skinner, Andrew and Thomas Wilson, eds (1975), *Essays on Adam Smith*, Oxford: Clarendon Press.

Teichgraber, Richard E., III (1986), *'Free Trade' and Moral Philosophy*, Durham: Duke University Press.

Viner, Jacob (1927), 'Adam Smith and Laissez Faire', *Journal of Political Economy*, **35**, pp. 198–214.

Waszek, Norbert (1984), 'Two Concepts of Morality: Adam Smith's Ethics and its Stoic Origins, *Journal of the History of Ideas*, **XLX**(4), pp. 591–606.

Winch, Donald (1978), *Adam Smith's Politics*, London: Cambridge University Press.

Winch, Donald (1992), 'Adam Smith: Scottish Moral Philosopher as Political Economist', *The Historical Journal*, **35**(1), pp. 91–113.

3 Adam Smith's unnaturally natural (yet naturally unnatural) use of the word 'natural'*

Spencer J. Pack

Natural and nature are complex words, fraught with ambiguity and contradiction. This paper does not attempt to give a complete account of Smith's use of these words. However, it does demonstrate that Smith did not necessarily approve of what he called 'natural' or 'nature'. Economists and others who assume otherwise are in error. A study, analysis, and/or interpretation of Smith's work which depends upon this (at times unstated) assumption – that Smith necessarily approved of 'nature' or the 'natural' – needs to be read with great care; perhaps even incredulity.[1]

Does 'natural' mean 'desirable'?

The impression has been given by various knowledgeable commentators of Adam Smith's work that Smith was unambiguously in favour of (or normatively disposed towards) what Smith called 'natural' or 'nature'. So, for example, Patricia Werhane in a recent extensive study of Smith's work writes that for Smith 'a society that emulates the system of *natural* liberty is most harmonious and closest to the *natural* order'; hence, for Smith 'the *natural* order of society is the ideal moral order'.[2]

Charles Clark, in a recent book lambasting 'natural law economics' for making economic thought ahistorical and asocial, writes that 'Smith's work was Newtonian because that was the best way of discovering the *natural* laws and God's design – the *natural* order'. For Smith 'God implanted in our *nature* drives and propensities which lead us to promote His end, which – since He is a benevolent God – is the well-being of society'. Clark claims that for Smith 'the basic idea behind the Invisible Hand is one of the major themes of *Natural* Theology: *nature* is arranged so as to provide for the prosperity and happiness of mankind, as long as man followed *nature's* design, the *natural* laws'.[3]

* An earlier version of this paper was presented at the History of Economics Society Meeting, 26–29 June 1993, Temple University, Philadelphia, Pennsylvania. I would like to thank Jolane Solomon, Dirk Held and Kenneth Bleeth for their help and comments. Responsibility for errors and opinions is entirely mine.

Jacob Viner in his classic article 'Adam Smith and Laissez Faire' wrote that 'Smith's major claim to fame ... seems to rest on his elaborate and detailed application to the economic world of the concept of a unified *natural* order, operating according to *natural* law, and if left to its own course producing results beneficial to mankind'. Viner explicitly reads Smith as associating the natural with good and the not natural with bad; hence, 'government activity is *natural* and therefore good where it promotes the general welfare, and is an interference with *nature* and therefore bad when it injures the general interests of society'.[4]

David McNally, in a recent detailed reinterpretation of Adam Smith and the classical political economists as exponents of a theory of 'agrarian capitalism'; argues that Smith 'saw these historical changes as creating a social relation (wage labour) consistent with the *natural* order of things and thus as indispensable to economic prosperity and social harmony'. McNally interprets Smith as having '*naturalized* and eternalized historically specific relations of production', thus giving Smith's work 'its uncritical and apologetic character'.[5]

These writers (as well as many others) have a tendency to misunderstand Smith, and mislead their readers, because they are insufficiently aware that Smith did not feel that what was 'natural' was necessarily desirable.[6]

This paper does not attempt a full analysis of Smith's promiscuous relationship with the words 'natural' and 'nature'.[7] Yet, it will be here noted that 'nature' and the 'natural' is an extraordinarily rich, complex, contradictory, no doubt dialectical concept.[8] C.S. Lewis in his *Studies in Words* says that 'nature' can mean, among other things, everything, or that which is created by God, or that which is sublunary, or the ordinary, or a thing's real character, or the actual, or the real, or the pre-civil, or that which is not touched by divine grace. Nature's opposite may be unnatural, artificial, not 'Man', not 'rational' law, supernatural, or towns.[9] Samuel Johnson's dictionary contains ten definitions for 'natural' and thirteen definitions for 'nature'.[10] It takes over four pages of small type for the *Oxford English Dictionary* to define 'natural'; and over two pages to define 'nature'.[11] It perhaps should not be expected that Smith should be entirely consistent in his use of such a pregnant term as 'nature' or 'natural'.[12] Nonetheless, I will now give examples where Smith used the words to describe something which he clearly did not approve of.

Let us begin with Smith's *Lectures on Jurisprudence*.[13] In a discussion of property rights, and means of acquiring property, in this case property by accession, Smith says:

> Among men too the child is considered as the property of the mother unless where she is the property of the husband, and then the offspring belongs to the father as an accession to the wife. This was the case in the old law in the state of wedlock

and in this point is still so, but *natural* children are the property of the mother and generally take her name.[14]

A natural child was one born of unwed parents. Smith wished to discourage the production of natural children.[15]

In lecturing on the transfer of property by succession, i.e. from the dead to the living, Smith says:

> Though when men get the power of conveying an estate by a testament they are often more willing to give their fortunes to those who are already rich, as they are their more respectable relations, than to those who are in lower circumstances. This perhaps is not altogether just but it is what men are *naturally* inclined to.[16]

It should be noted here Smith makes an invidious comparison between what is perhaps 'altogether just' and that which men are 'naturally' inclined to do. Clearly, Smith does not necessarily favour what men are 'naturally' inclined to do.

In a discussion of earlier times, Smith describes how the barbarous nations of the north overran the Roman empire, the arts were neglected, and a great share of power went into the hands of those who possessed the greatest property. Smith says that in his contemporary society 'A tradesman to retain your custom may perhaps vote for you in an election, but you need not expect that he will attend you to battle'.[17]

> As the dependents were in every respect so entirely maintained by these allodiall lords (as they were called) for maintainance and every thing they enjoyed, it was *natural* that they should attend him in war and defend him when injured by the other lords or their dependents. And they were constantly about him, whether in peace or in war; in peace they were entertained at his table, and in war they were his soldiers.[18]

Smith is here describing a relationship which was 'natural'; yes, natural given the socioeconomic arrangements at the time. Yet, note: this is exactly the type of 'natural' personal servile relationship which vexed Smith deeply.[19] For Smith, 'Nothing tends so much to corrupt and enervate and debase the mind as dependency, and nothing gives such noble and generous notions of probity as freedom and independency.'[20]

In discussing slavery Smith says: 'It is to be observed that slavery takes place in all societies at their beginning, and proceeds from that tyrannic disposition which may almost be said to be *natural* to mankind.'[21]

For people who think that Smith was some kind of Panglossian optimist, his views on slavery make sobering reading. Smith doubted that slavery would 'ever be totally or generally abolished'.[22] Smith says of slavery in a free country that the love of domination and authority and the pleasure men take in having every thing done by their express orders, rather than to condescend to bargain and treat with those whom they look upon as their inferiors and are inclined to use in a haughty way; this love of domination and tyrannizing, I say, will make it impossible for the slaves in a free country ever to recover their liberty.[23]

A little later, in discussing the situation of the coal miners in his time, Smith says that it is in the narrow economic interests of the masters of coal works to free their miners, who are kept in virtual slavery.

[O]ne who works a year and day in the coal pit becomes a slave as the rest and may be claimed by the owner, unless he has bargained not to take advantage of this. But this the masters of coal works will never agree to. The love of domination and authority over others, which I am afraid is *natural* to mankind, a certain desire of having others below one, and the pleasure it gives one to have some persons whom he can order to do his work rather than be obliged to persuade others to bargain with him, will for ever hinder this from taking place.[24]

Smith deeply desires a social system to be set up, which is structured so that it minimizes the ability of the powerful to use personal domination and authority over others and to tyrannize their underlings. In the above particular situation, if the superiors in question freed their coal miners, wages would fall; coal owners in effect pay a premium so as to be able to have the coal workers in slavery.[25] Note how Smith wants to develop social institutions to counteract a 'natural' human inclination: the love of personal domination and authority over others.

In a similar vein concerning 'natural' human passions which are undesirable, Smith says: 'Treasure and derelict goods by the laws of Britain belong to the king. This arises from that *natural* influence of superiors which draws every thing to itself that it can without a violation of the most manifest rules of justice.'[26]

This is reminiscent of a point Smith made on the proper subjects of tragedies in his *Lectures on Rhetoric and Belles Lettres*. There he says that 'There is in human *nature* a servility which inclines us to adore our superiors and an inhumanity which disposes us to contemn and trample under foot our inferiors.'[27]

Note how in the same sentence Smith attributes an inhumanity to *human nature*.

In the 'Early Draft of Part of *The Wealth of Nations*', Smith writes of a 'greediness which is *natural* to man'.[28] Smith's use of the word natural in connection with greediness (which he does not approve of) occurs in the context of outlining how political rulers seize all vacant lands as soon as the idea of private property in land is introduced. This seizure inhibits the slow progress of opulence; naturally, Smith denounces it.[29]

Returning to the *Lectures on Jurisprudence*, Smith discusses war between nations, and comments upon guilt by association: 'We have been injured by France, our resentment rises against the whole nation instead of the government, and they, through a blind indiscriminating faculty *natural* to mankind, become the objects of an unreasonable resentment.'[30] Smith is against this 'unreasonable' resentment; it is 'quite contrary to the rules of justice observed with regard to our own subjects'.[31] Unfortunately, 'in war there must always be the greatest injustice but it is inevitable'.[32] Inevitable, perhaps; yet, Smith clearly does not approve of this injustice which results from a *natural* indiscriminating human faculty.

Smith discusses the development of money as a universal equivalent. 'In Italy, and particularly in Tuscany, every thing was compared with sheep, as this was their principal commodity. This is what may be called the *natural* measure of value.'[33] Notice how a 'natural' measure of value arose at a certain level of socioeconomic development. Smith discusses how money developed from cattle and oxen and sheep to the precious metals. Gold and silver became the measure of value:

> In the same manner as they changed the *natural* measures of length into artificial ones, so did they those of value. All measures were originally taken from the human body; a fathom was measured by the stretch of a man's arms, a yard was the half of this, a span an inch or digit, ... These *natural* measures could not long satisfy them, as these would vary greatly, ... Prudent men therefore contrived, and the public established, artificial yards, fathoms, feet, inches, etc. which should be the measures of all different lengths. For the same reason they converted the original and *natural* measures of value into others not so *natural*, but more convenient than any of those *naturally* used by men in the ruder ages of society.[34]

Smith favoured the development away from a more 'natural' measure of value to the precious metals. 'The *natural* measures of sheep or oxen would not answer their purpose; a more precise measure was requisite, the value of which could always be ascertained by its quantity.'[35] People became more careful in their trades and 'bargains'; the 'natural' measure of value was rightfully superseded. After all, as Smith patiently explains, it would indeed be 'a very great hardship on a Glasgow merchant to give him a cow for one of his commodities'.[36]

'Natural habits'
In the so-called 'History of Astronomy' essay,[37] in a discussion of the origin of philosophy, Smith writes that 'in the first ages of society ... cowardice and pusillanimity, so *natural* to man in his uncivilized state ... unprotected by the laws of society, exposed, defenceless, he feels his weakness upon all occasions; his strength and security upon none'.[38]

For Smith, cowardice and pusillanimity are *natural* to man in the early stages of society. W.P.D. Whightman, Smith's rather quarrelsome modern editor of the majority of his *Essays on Philosophical Subjects* [39] writes that 'Smith seems to have had an obsession about "cowards"'.[40] Smith, of course, was against cowardice and pusillanimity. One of his major concerns in the *Lectures on Jurisprudence* was how to defend society.[41] Smith deals with this issue in *The Wealth of Nations*, in Book V, Chapter I, Part I, 'Of the Expence of Defence'. Here, among other things, Smith claims that 'An industrious, and upon that account a wealthy nation, is of all nations the most likely to be attacked; and unless the state takes some new measures for the public defence, the *natural* habits of the people render them altogether incapable of defending themselves'.[42] According to Smith, due to the 'natural' social habits engendered in a commercial (or capitalist) society, the state of a commercial society must spend the money to maintain a standing army. In this passage, coming as it does in the middle of a discussion comparing the warlike qualities of people in hunting, shepherding, farming and commercial societies, it is clear that Smith is dealing with 'natural habits' which are, indeed, socially determined by the level of society. Moreover, Smith does not entirely approve of all of these 'natural habits'. Some of these undesirable 'natural habits' require the attention of the state.

Natural profligacy
In the *Wealth of Nations* in discussing the advantages of the division of labour and specialization, Smith writes that

> The habit of sauntering and of indolent careless application, which is *naturally*, or rather necessarily acquired by every country workman who is obliged to change his work and his tools every half hour, and to apply his hand in twenty different ways almost every day of his life; renders him almost always slothful and lazy, and incapable of any vigorous application even on the most pressing occasions.[43]

As might be expected, Smith is against the sloth and laziness 'natural' to the country workman.

In discussing wages, Smith notes that 'We rarely hear, it has been said, of the combinations of masters ... because it is the usual, and one may say, the *natural* state of things which nobody ever hears of'.[44] Smith was against combinations of masters; he disapproved of this 'natural state'.

Smith writes that 'entails are the *natural* consequences of the law of primogeniture'.[45] Primogeniture is the right of the eldest child, especially the eldest son, to inherit the entire estate of one or both parents; entails on land were rules by which the inheritance to the land in future generations was fixed. Smith was against both of them.

In a chapter arguing against government deficit spending Smith writes, 'In a commercial country abounding with every sort of expensive luxury, the sovereign, in the same manner as almost all the great proprietors in his dominions *naturally* spends a great part of his revenue in purchasing those luxuries'.[46] Smith argued against this sort of 'natural' profligate government spending since, among other reasons, 'The want of parsimony in time of peace, imposes the necessity of contracting debt in time of war'.[47]

The nature of human affairs

In a discussion of what Smith perceived to be a contemporary stationary state, Smith writes that 'China seems to have been long stationary, and had probably long ago acquired that full complement of riches which is consistent with the *nature* of its laws and institutions'.[48] Hence, human laws and institutions can have a 'nature'; and Smith disapproved of some of those laws and institutions. In particular, if China opened up more to foreign commerce, and gave greater security to the poor and the owners of small capital, then it could break out of the stationary state and increase its wealth.

Immediately before explaining that 'the mean rapacity, the monopolizing spirit of merchants and manufacturers, who neither are, nor ought to be the rulers of mankind ... may very easily be prevented from disturbing the tranquillity of any body but themselves' Smith comments that 'the violence and injustice of the rulers of mankind is an ancient evil, for which, I am afraid, the *nature* of human affairs can scarce admit of a remedy'.[49] Here is a situation in which the 'nature' of human affairs can do little to remedy an ancient evil. Although the word 'evil' is one which has generally dropped out of twentieth-century economists' discourse, I think it is clear enough that Smith was against this sort of 'evil' engendered by the nature of human affairs.

In Book IV, at the end of the long chapter 'Of Colonies', after a description castigating how the East India Company is ruining India, Smith writes,

> I mean not, however, by any thing which I have said, to throw any odious imputation upon the general character of the servants of the East India company, and much less upon that of any particular persons. It is the system of government, the situation in which they are placed, that I mean to censure; not the character of those who have acted on it. They acted as their situation *naturally* directed, ...[50]

Here the stewards in the East India Company acted in a 'natural' way, based upon their position in a mercantile monopoly which was also the sovereign of a country. This was a 'natural' way which Smith disapproved of. He disapproved of a monopolist mercantile firm being the sovereign of a country and the 'natural' consequences which follow from it.

Smith returns to the theme of monopolies in Book V, and elaborates on how they attempt to restrict output and increase prices: 'The usual corporation spirit, wherever the law does not restrain it, prevails in all regulated companies. When they have been allowed to act according to their *natural* genius, they have always, in order to confine the competition to as small a number of persons as possible, ...'.[51] Attempts to restrict competition is exactly the sort of 'natural genius' which Smith most vehemently attacked.

Later in the same article, near the end of a very long paragraph outlining the disgraceful history of the English East India Company, Smith writes:

> No other sovereigns ever were, or, from the *nature* of things, ever could be, so perfectly indifferent about the happiness or misery of their subjects, the improvement or waste of their dominions, the glory or disgrace of their administration; as, from irresistible moral causes, the greater part of the proprietors of such a mercantile company are, and necessarily must be.[52]

These are the 'nature of things', the irresistible moral causes which result when a monopolist, mercantile company is the sovereign of a country; Smith was against this sort of nature.[53]

In the next article, in dealing with managerial problems in controlling college professors, Smith argues that professors should be at least partly paid for by the students themselves. If professors are not, and they are responsible to authorities outside the university, such as a bishop or a governor or a minister, there will be administrative difficulties:

> An extraneous jurisdiction of this kind, besides, is liable to be exercised both ignorantly and capriciously. In its *nature* it is arbitrary and discretionary, and the persons who exercise it, neither attending upon the lectures of the teacher themselves, nor perhaps understanding the sciences which it is his business to teach, are seldom capable of exercising it with judgment. ... Whoever has attended for any considerable time to the administration of a French university, must have had occasion to remark the effects which *naturally* result from an arbitrary and extraneous jurisdiction of this kind.[54]

Of course, Smith is against authority which is of its nature ignorant, arbitrary and capricious.[55]

Later in the same article, Smith deals with the deleterious effects of the division of labour on the mind and character of the worker in commercial (capitalist) society. According to Smith, the worker '*naturally* loses, therefore, the habit of such exertion, and generally becomes as stupid and ignorant as it is possible for a human creature to become'.[56] Smith is against work-induced stupidity and ignorance which 'naturally' arises from the division of labour in commercial societies. He argues that the government should use education to try to counteract these undesirable 'natural' traits.

Summary and conclusion

Greater study and care needs to be devoted to how Smith uses the words 'natural' and 'nature'. These are complex words, fraught with ambiguity. The present paper has proposed to demonstrate that Smith did not necessarily approve of 'nature' or of things which he denoted as 'natural'. Yet, the paper's implications may possibly be far-reaching. Economists and others who assume that Smith necessarily approved of 'nature' or what is 'natural' are in error. A rereading of Smith with this point in mind may be warranted.

Notes

1. This paper is part of a series of papers I am working on concerning Smith's methodology and world view. My reading of Smith is that he is an epistemological sceptic; concerning human nature he is an ontological pessimist; Smith did not unambiguously believe in 'progress' or that humans can approach 'truth': hence the importance of rhetoric in his thought (see e.g. Griswold, 1991); Smith's analyses were generally historically specific (see e.g. Pack, 1993; also Cremaschi, 1981). Smith's promiscuous use (by today's standards) of the words 'nature' and 'natural' has tended to obscure the fact that his analyses were neither asocial nor ahistorical; nor were they uncritical of commercial or capitalist society.

2. Werhane (1991), pp. 82, 50, emphasis added.

3. Clark (1992) pp. 42, 48, emphasis added. See also Clark (1989; 1990). That this seems to be an oversimplification of Smith's theological views see e.g. Pack (1992).

4. Viner (1928) pp. 118, 141, emphasis added.

5. McNally (1988), p. 261, emphasis added. For interpretations that Smith's work was neither apologetic nor uncritical see e.g. Rothschild (1992), Pack (1991).

6. For other prominent examples of this problem see e.g. Veblen (1948) and Marx (1963), Chap. 2, 'Seventh and Last Observation'.

7. The most profound reflections on the use of 'nature' and 'natural' in Smith's work are perhaps in Cremaschi (1989). Cremaschi argues that Smith used 'nature' and 'natural' as a metaphysical link between 'reality' or 'truth' which, following Hume, Smith felt he was unable to know or appropriate or make 'progress' towards, and historicism. Hence, talk of nature and the natural provided Smith with a buffer or bridge between 'the individual mind and the ultimate order of reality' (p. 104). Indeed, it is 'true' that Smith rarely if ever talks of, e.g. 'the progress of truth' (Stewart, 1980, p. 327) or if something is truthful. Smith does talk incessantly about the nature of a thing and if something is natural.

8. See e.g. Freud (1963), 'The Antithetical Sense of Primal Words', pp. 44–50; Hegel (1967), 'Perception: Or Things and Their Deceptiveness', pp. 161–78. Indeed, if there is some sort of dialectical unfolding of human history, or if there is any 'truth' to 'Freudian slips' and Freud's concern that 'we should understand the language of dreams better and translate it more easily if we knew more about the development of language' (Freud, 1963, p. 50) then it should be particularly reflected in the history and development of the use of the words nature and natural, and their synonyms and antonyms. The proper understanding of texts by economists could be enhanced by attention to the field of historical linguistics. This field, of course, was a keen interest of Smith's; see, e.g. 'Considerations Concerning the First Formation of Languages' in Smith (1983).

9. Lewis (1967), Chap. 2, 'Nature (With Phusis, Kind, Physical etc.)', pp. 24–74. Its opposite can also be revealed, as in revealed theology.

10. Smith wrote an influential review of Johnson's dictionary for the *Edinburgh Review*. See Smith (1980), pp. 229–41.

11. A few years ago I asked the curator of the Peabody Museum of Natural History at Yale University to define 'natural' for me. He could not. I asked him then how he could decide what belonged in a museum of natural history and what did not. His answer was exceedingly complex; in fact, I was unable to decipher it.

12. For an example of, e.g., Smith's rather loose translating style, compare his translation of extracts from Rousseau's *Discours sur l'origine et les fondemens de l'inegalité parmi les hommes* with the original in Smith (1980) pp. 251–6.

 Puro (1992) gives examples of eight distinct usages of the term 'natural' in *The Wealth of Nations*.

13. Smith's *Lectures on Jurisprudence*, especially his more recently discovered 'Report of 1762–3', have not received the attention they deserve from Smith scholars. These lectures reveal a deep historical depth to Smith, as well as an affinity with Marx. See Meek (1977).

14. Smith (1978), p. 27, emphasis added.

15. See, e.g. ibid., pp. 447–8.

16. Ibid., p. 40, emphasis added.

17. Ibid., p. 50.

18. Ibid., p. 51, emphasis added.

19. See, e.g. Perelman (1989).

20. Smith (1978), p. 333.

21. Ibid., p. 452, emphasis added.

22. Ibid., p. 181.

23. Ibid., p. 186.

24. Ibid., p. 192, emphasis added.

25. Ibid.

26. Ibid., p. 460, emphasis added.

27. Smith (1983), p. 124, emphasis added.

28. Smith (1978), p. 579, emphasis added.

29. It also introduces the concept of monopoly rent which creates havoc with Smith's theory of price determination. See Ricardo (1977), Dmitriev (1974).

30. Smith (1978), p. 547, emphasis added.

31. Ibid.

32. Ibid., p. 548.

33. Ibid., p. 499, emphasis added.

34. Ibid., pp. 367–8, emphasis added.

35. Ibid., pp. 368–9, emphasis added.

36. Ibid., p. 500.

37. This and the 'History of the Ancient Physics' and the 'History of the Ancient Logics and Metaphysics' are each preceded by the title 'The Principles which Lead and Direct Philosophical Enquiries'. Thus, each of these pieces appear to be actually part of a larger, unified, unfinished essay of that name. The traditional nomenclature emphasizes viewing these pieces as separate histories, rather than as pieces of a unitary essay on methodology. This nomenclature has the tendency to obscure the importance of these essays for understanding Smith's methodology.

38. Smith (1980), p. 48, emphasis added.

39. 'At this stage some readers may reasonably protest that it is an editor's function at most to comment on the text and not to argue with its author' (Wightman, 1980, p. 25). Quite true.

40. Smith (1980), p. 168, n.35.

41. Particularly calamitous in Smith's view is when a society based upon an 'earlier' or 'more primitive' stage of development, such as a shepherding society, overruns a more 'advanced' or 'sophisticated' society such as one based upon farming or commerce. Arguably, the importance of Smith's concern has been highlighted in recent years by such events as the destruction wreaked by the backwards Khmer Rouge in Kampuchea and the contemporary so-called 'ethnic cleansing' by the rude (primitive, relatively undeveloped) Serbs in Bosnia Herzegovina.

42. *WN*, V.i.a.15, emphasis added.

43. *WN*, I.i.7, emphasis added.

44. *WN*, I.viii,13, emphasis added.

45. *WN*, III.ii.5, emphasis added.

46. *WN*, V.iii.3, emphasis added.

47. *WN*, V.iii.4.

48. *WN*, I.ix.15, emphasis added.
49. *WN*, IV.iii.c.9, emphasis added.
50. *WN*, IV.vii.c.107, emphasis added.
51. *WN*, V.i.e.7, emphasis added.
52. *WN*, V.i.e.26, emphasis added.
53. For someone who used Smith's name to argue in favour of mercantile rule, see Stigler (1988). This truly disheartening misuse of Smith's name by someone who clearly knew better was peddled to the apparently unsuspecting philistines in the National Association of Business Economists. As Galbraith (1992) has pointed out, Smith was 'deeply averse to joint stock companies, now called corporations ... Modern advocates of free enterprise would find Smith's attack on corporations deeply disconcerting.' (pp. 99–100)
54. *WN*, V.i.f.9, emphasis added.
55. The accuracy of Smith's characterization of French universities is not currently at issue.
56. *WN*, V.i.f.50, emphasis added.

References
Clark, Charles M.A. (1989), 'Natural Law Influences on Adam Smith', *Quaderni di Storia dell'Economia Politica*, **6**, Winter, pp. 59–86.
Clark, Charles M.A. (1990), 'Adam Smith and Society as an Evolutionary Process', *Journal of Economics Issues*, **24**(3), pp. 825–44.
Clark, Charles M.A. (1992), *Economic Theory and Natural Philosophy*, Aldershot: Edward Elgar.
Cremaschi, Sergio (1981), 'Adam Smith, Newtonianism and Political Economy', *Manuscrito*, **5**(1), pp. 117–34.
Cremaschi, Sergio (1989), 'Adam Smith: Skeptical Newtonianism, Disenchanted Republicanism, and the Birth of Social Science', in Marcelo Dascal and Ora Gruengard, eds, *Knowledge and Politics: Case Studies in the Relationship Between Epistemology and Political Philosophy*, Boulder, CO: Westview Press.
Dmitriev, V.K. (1974), *Economic Essays on Value, Competition and Utility*, Cambridge: Cambridge University Press.
Freud, Sigmund (1963), *Character and Culture*, New York: Collier Books.
Galbraith, John Kenneth (1992), *The Culture of Contentment*, Boston: Houghton Mifflin Company.
Griswold, Charles L. Jr (1991), 'Rhetoric and Ethics: Adam Smith on Theorizing about the Moral Sentiments', *Philosophy and Rhetoric*, **24**(3), pp. 213–37.
Hegel, G.W.F. (1967), *The Phenomenology of Mind*, New York: Harper and Row.
Lewis, C.S. (1967), *Studies in Words*, 2nd ed., Cambridge: Cambridge University Press.
Marx, Karl (1963), *The Poverty of Philosophy*, New York: International Publishers.
McNally, David (1988), *Political Economy and the Rise of Capitalism: A Reinterpretation*, Berkeley: University of California Press.
Meek, Ronald (1977), *Smith, Marx, and After*, New York: John Wiley and Sons.
Pack, Spencer J. (1991), *Capitalism as a Moral System: Adam Smith's Critique of the Free Market Economy*, Aldershot: Edward Elgar.
Pack, Spencer J. (1992), 'Theological (and hence Economic) Implications of Adam Smith's The Principles which Lead and Direct Philosophical Enquiries''', paper presented to the History of Economic Thought Conference, George Mason University, Fairfax, VA, May–June 1992.
Pack, Spencer J. (1993), 'Adam Smith on the Limits to Human Reason', in Robert F. Hébert, ed., *Perspectives on the History of Economic Thought: Selected Papers from the History of Economic Thought Conference 1991, Volume IX*, Aldershot: Edward Elgar.
Perelman, Michael (1989), 'Adam Smith and Dependent Social Relations', *History of Political Economy*, **21**(3), pp. 503–20.
Puro, Edward (1992), 'Uses of the Term "Natural" in Adam Smith's *Wealth of Nations*', *Research in the History of Economic Thought and Methodology*, **9**, pp. 73–86.
Ricardo, David (1977), *The Principles of Political Economy and Taxation*, New York: Dutton.

Rothschild, Emma (1992), 'Adam Smith and Conservative Economics', *Economic History Review*, **XLV**(I), pp. 74–96.

Smith, Adam (1976), *An Inquiry into the Nature and Causes of the Wealth of Nations*, ed. R.H. Campbell and A.S. Skinner, Oxford: Oxford University Press.

Smith, Adam (1978), *Lectures on Jurisprudence*, ed. R.L. Meek, D.D. Raphael and P.G. Stein, Oxford: Oxford University Press.

Smith, Adam (1980), *Essays on Philosophical Subjects*, ed. W.P.D. Wightman and J.C. Bryce, Oxford: Oxford University Press.

Smith, Adam (1983), *Lectures on Rhetoric and Belles Lettres*, ed. J.C. Bryce, Oxford: Oxford University Press.

Stewart, Dugald (1980), 'Account of the Life and Writings of Adam Smith', in Adam Smith, *Essays on Philosophical Subjects*, Oxford: Oxford University Press, pp. 269–351.

Stigler, George (1988), 'The Adam Smith Lecture: The Effect of Government on Economic Efficiency', *Business Economics*, **23**(1), pp. 7–13.

Veblen, Thorstein (1948), 'The Preconceptions of the Classical Economists', in Marx Lerner, ed., *The Portable Veblen*, New York: The Viking Press, pp. 241–74.

Viner, Jacob (1928), 'Adam Smith and Laissez Faire' in John Maurice Clark et al., *Adam Smith 1776–1926*, Chicago: University of Chicago Press, pp. 116–55.

Werhane, Patricia (1991), *Adam Smith and His Legacy for Modern Capitalism*, Oxford: Oxford University Press.

Wightman, W.P.D. (1980), 'Introduction' in Adam Smith, *Essays on Philosophical Subjects*, ed. W.P.D. Wightman and J.C. Bryce, Oxford: Oxford University Press, pp. 5–27.

4 A game-theoretic re-evaluation of Adam Smith's *Theory of Moral Sentiments* and *Wealth of Nations*

Andreas Ortmann and Stephen Meardon

Abstract

We explain in the following paper how, in more lengthy studies, we have applied elementary concepts of game theory to illustrate a basic incentive problem running through Smith's work. The incentive problem is the tension between individual and aggregate rationality, or between short-term and long-term rationality. It arises in three contexts, providing the bases for the three papers informing this survey: the individual's struggle to acquire self-command (Meardon and Ortmann, 1995a), the evolution of moral standards through interaction of many people (Ortmann and Meardon, 1995), and problems of externalities and provision of public goods (Meardon and Ortmann, 1995b). After reviewing the arguments of the three papers, we use them to form conclusions regarding the relationship of *The Theory of Moral Sentiments* to *The Wealth of Nations* and the validity of the historical treatment of Smith as an analytical economist.

Introduction

In the following pages we uncover the basic incentive problem underlying Adam Smith's *Theory of Moral Sentiments* (*TMS*) and *Wealth of Nations* (*WN*). We show that the problem can be framed as what we call the 'Smith game', a generic term for (symmetric) hawk–dove games and (asymmetric) reputation games and variants thereof. In one-shot situations the Smith game features the tension between individual and aggregate rationality leading to the Pareto-inefficient outcomes characteristic of prisoners' dilemma games. However, under standard assumptions, when repeated indefinitely the Smith game can result in Pareto-efficient outcomes.

We have shown elsewhere in detailed studies how Smith used the reputation version of his game in *TMS* to model the acquisition of self-command *given general rules of morality* (Meardon and Ortmann, 1995a). We have also shown how he used the hawk–dove version of his game in *TMS* to model the origin and evolution of general rules of morality (Ortmann and Meardon, 1995), and how his game underlies a variety of central problem isomorphs in

WN, particularly (but not exclusively) those found in Book V (Meardon and Ortmann, 1995b).

In this paper we paint the big picture. First, we review the application of the Smith game to *TMS* and *WN* in our three detailed studies. Our approach suggests that Smith – while he did not use these terms – understood well and dealt with the pervasive nature of externalities and the related issue of reputational enforcement. The latter two issues, brought into sharp focus through the conceptual lenses of game theory and growing evidence supplied by experimental economics, are nowadays the major concerns of practitioners of a wide variety of economic sub-disciplines: from modern microeconomic theory to modern macroeconomic policy and the political economy of institutions and decisions.[1] Second, we explain why recognition of the incentive problem modelled by the Smith game is crucial for an understanding of *TMS* and *WN* and their relation to each other. In doing so we find our approach can contribute to the discussion of the 'Adam Smith problem', the notion that Smith's thoughts in *TMS* and *WN* are incongruous or disjointed. Finally, having uncovered the tools of analysis that Smith employed implicitly more than two hundred years ago, we revisit the question of whether or not Smith was an analytical economist.

We use some standard assumptions, tools, and results of game theory in making our arguments – particularly the difference, for certain classes of games, between the outcomes of one-shot and indefinitely repeated games under the employment of trigger strategies. Those who are not familiar with the assumptions, tools, and results of game theory that we use throughout the paper might find useful the review of selected concepts of game theory included as an appendix.

Acquisition of self-command in *The Theory of Moral Sentiments*
In *TMS* Smith frames the acquisition of individual self-command as a struggle between two 'selves' with different preferences. The two selves emerge in any situation where a person must choose how to act while under the influence of some emotion or 'passion'. These selves may be called the 'Man Yesterday' and the 'Man Today'. Smith thought of the Man Yesterday as a person inflamed by passion, and the Man Today as the same person after his passion has subsided. In our game-theoretic formulation the Man Yesterday is still the person inflamed by passion, but the Man Today is now both a real person existing after the Man Yesterday, and an imaginary construct in the Man Yesterday's mind. This interpretation captures the simultaneous struggle Smith envisioned, and rationalizes the assumption of simultaneity to be made once the game is set up.

> At the very time of acting, at the moment in which passion mounts the highest, [the man of furious resentment] hesitates and trembles at the thought of what he is

about to do: he is secretly conscious to himself that he is breaking through those measures of conduct which, in all his cool hours, he had resolved never to infringe, which he had never seen infringed by others without the highest disapprobation, and of which the infringement, his own mind forebodes, must soon render him the object of the same disagreeable sentiments. Before he can take the last fatal resolution, he is tormented with all the agonies of doubt and uncertainty; he is terrified at the thought of violating so sacred a rule, and at the same time is urged and goaded on by the fury of his desires to violate it. (*TMS*, p. 161)

Smith held the view that a person inflamed by passion is nevertheless aware, to some extent, of the impropriety of the action he is considering and its possible consequences to his future state of mind. At the moment of choice a struggle for dominance erupts in his mind between his passionate self and his prudent self – 'his own mind forebodes'. The Man Yesterday is urged by his passion, but is also influenced by his thoughts of a more prudent self who would be concerned with the ultimate effects of the action after the passion has subsided. The more prudent self is the Man Today, whose feelings are partially, though not wholly, internalized by the Man Yesterday.

Payoffs in this game are determined primarily by feelings of praise-worthiness and blame-worthiness. Smith tells us these feelings are indeed motives for actions; rational, self-interested people will act generously, benevolently, etc. in order to generate feelings of praise-worthiness and avoid feelings of blame-worthiness. The beneficent man Smith describes at many points in *TMS* is rarely a genuine altruist. His payoffs include the feelings generated by his actions, and he is motivated to act by these payoffs. Thus even though emotions play a major role in determining the outcome of the game – since they *are* payoffs – choices are nevertheless made rationally. By choosing his action, a player chooses the set of emotions he may possibly feel as a result of the action. It is reasonable to assume he will choose the action that will be likely to lead him to feel better than he would if he chose any other action. Even though his *payoffs* are in the realm of emotions, his *decisions* are rational in the sense of payoff maximizing. Our approach thus illuminates Smith's (partial) endorsement of the rational actor paradigm.

The Man Yesterday faces two choices: to act properly or to act improperly, where standards of propriety are assumed to be predetermined and known.[2] His payoffs are maximized in a one-shot game by succumbing to his passions and acting improperly – particularly if his actions will not be carefully evaluated. The choices of the Man Today, on the other hand, are to evaluate the action of the Man Yesterday only casually, or to evaluate it deeply and carefully. We call the former a routine evaluation and the latter a real evaluation.[3] Real evaluation is costly (in terms of blame-worthiness and time and effort, which are also components of the payoffs), so the Man Today would prefer to routinely evaluate a proper action by the Man Yesterday. Given that the Man Yesterday acts improperly, however, the Man Today would prefer to make a real evaluation. He knows it is costly and will make him feel blame-worthy for what was done, but he also knows that it might prevent the 'Yesterday' self from acting similarly in the future, and thus ensures that he will not need to feel blame-worthy again. Furthermore he feels praise-worthy for incurring the momentary pain of self-evaluation for the sake of future self-command, and this feeling of praise-worthiness outweighs the feeling of blame-worthiness.

The game is set up, and the payoffs might be illustrated, as in Figure 4.1

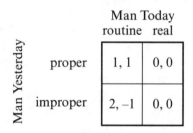

Figure 4.1   The Smith game of self-command acquisition

In a one-shot game both players will choose the 'defect' strategy (in this case meaning the improper choice by the Man Yesterday, and the choice of real evaluation by the Man Today). If the world ended tomorrow the Man Yesterday would have fewer reservations about acting improperly, because there could be no long-run gains from acting properly. And with no estab-lished habit of the Man Yesterday acting properly, or giving any indication of doing so, the Man Today would be inclined to make a real evaluation of his actions. Thus a one-shot play of the game ends in the lower right corner of the payoff table (Figure 4.1) a sub-optimal Nash equilibrium – neither player would change his decision unilaterally even if given the opportunity.

If the players know the game will be repeated indefinitely, however, the outcome changes. Each player knows that his choice in each round of the game affects his payoffs in future rounds as well. Assuming the Man Yester-day has reason to believe the Man Today will use the trigger strategy, the Man Yesterday will not want to choose the improper action because he knows the outcome will be confined to the lower right corner, and his payoff re-stricted to zero, forever after. Intuitively, the trigger strategy is the Man Today continuously making the real evaluation in response to an improper action because he can't depend on any habit of 'real constancy and firmness' (*TMS*, p. 146) on the part of the Man Yesterday. The Man Yesterday will not want to subject himself always to the fiercest mental struggles represented by the lower right corner when instead he can establish a habit of acting properly, and thereby ensure himself long-term positive payoffs (feelings of praise-worthiness).[4]

This model of the acquisition of self-command clarifies an important point in *TMS*: for a well-defined class of passions no commitment device or third-party enforcement is necessary to ensure that people will meet the standards of propriety, or abide by the general rules of morality (we use these terms synonymously).[5] It is not necessarily an ingrained sense of altruism that brings people to use self-command – to choose beneficence and generosity, or at least justice, over acts of hatred, resentment, and the like. They may do so self-interestedly, to maximize their own payoffs, when self-interest is defined broadly and payoffs are in part determined by feelings of praise-worthiness and blame-worthiness.

On the origin and evolution of moral sentiments

In our exhibition of Smith's model of acquisition of self-command, we treated the general rules of morality as given; this was done for ease of exposition and to establish a benchmark. In Ortmann and Meardon (1995), we have suggested how Smith modelled the evolution of moral sentiments, i.e. the development of the general rules themselves. For this purpose Smith implic-itly used hawk–dove-type games, played repeatedly by members of society as they interact with one another; their choices are to abide by or to disregard the moral standards. A two-person hawk–dove game – specifically, a prison-er's dilemma game – is presented in the appendix. The extension to an *n*-person game, which must be used to model the evolution of societal stand-ards, is straightforward.[6]

We discuss this, and other extensions (different strategies, noise, restric-tions on computational ability) more fully in Ortmann and Meardon (1995). There we also review the current discourse on 'eductive' and 'evolutive' modelling efforts which have led to interesting insights about the relation between static and dynamic equilibrium notions and the origin and evolution of conventions.[7]

Regarding the terms 'eductive' and 'evolutive', Binmore explains:

> The word *eductive* will be used to describe a dynamic process by means of which equilibrium is achieved through careful reasoning on the part of the players. Such reasoning will usually require an attempt to simulate the reasoning process of the other players. ... The word *evolutive* will be used to describe a dynamic process by means of which equilibrium is achieved through evolutionary mechanisms. ... adjustment takes place as a result of *iterated* play by *myopic* players. (1990, p. 155)

Among the major results of the current discourse is the insight that the predictions of the eductive and evolutive approaches may diverge for important classes of games. This bears directly on the outcome of the game we uncover in Ortmann and Meardon (1995): the Smith game of the evolution of moral sentiments.

Smith had no doubt that 'the general maxims of morality are formed, like all other general maxims, from experience and induction' (*TMS*, p. 319). In the Smith game of the evolution of moral sentiments this would suggest players' strategies are developed evolutively. The problem is that a player whose strategy develops evolutively has not, for whatever reason, been able to determine in advance that a strategy of abiding strictly to the moral standards (wherever that moving target may be at the time) is in his long-run best interest. Forming a strategy evolutively is the choice by default of a player who doesn't have the ability to form one eductively. The ability to form a strategy eductively depends on whether the player possesses certain other abilities: the ability to observe and recall behavior of others, computational ability, and the ability to gauge the 'payoffs' that future interactions promise. Any player who does not have these abilities in abundance – for example a child, or a person without 'real constancy and firmness' – must form his strategy evolutively instead. As he gropes his way, evolutively, towards a consistent strategy, he is likely to behave below the moral standards at times – having the external effect of lowering the standards themselves. This could lead to a tearing of the social fabric, and possibly call for preventive or corrective measures by the state.

If, on the other hand, strategies were somehow developed eductively, strict moral standards and a strong social fabric might prevail without the intervention of government. Players could see in advance that abiding consistently by the moral standards is a strategy not only optimal for society, but optimal for themselves in the long run. The standards would then be met, and possibly even raised. Smith's frequent displays in both *TMS* and *WN* of what we call his 'Newtonian' view of the world – the notion that all of the universe, even down to the sentiments of man, functions as a great machine powered by the will of the Deity and moving towards a grand design – would seem to suggest players' strategies should actually be thought of as being formed eductively.

Smith seems to have become more pessimistic in the course of his life of the probability of moral standards converging (without the aid of a third party) toward the will of the Deity – suggesting that in his later years the evolutive approach seemed to him to be more realistic.[8] Some form of government intervention might therefore be called for to put moral standards on the correct path. In fact, this rationale underlies Smith's call for government involvement in provision of a public good that helps players choose their strategies in the game just discussed. As we shall soon see, that particular public good is education.

A game-theoretic interpretation of *The Wealth of Nations*
We begin our modelling of the incentive problems in *WN* with an example from Book I that Smith believed a free market resolves satisfactorily. We then move on to those he believed the free market leaves unresolved.

In *WN*, Book I, Chapter VIII, 'Of the Wages of Labour', Smith's discussion could be treated in game-theoretic form as an 'efficiency wage' game.[9] He writes '(w)here wages are high, accordingly, we shall always find the workmen more active, diligent, and expeditious, than where they are low; ...' (*WN*, p. 81).

The game pits employers against employees. The employer can pay a premium for high-quality work or can pay the standard wage. The employee can work hard or slack off. In each case the first choice is cooperative (proper) and the second non-cooperative (improper). The resultant set-up is a standard principal-agent game which we have used in Meardon and Ortmann (1995a) to represent Smith's model of the acquisition of self-command. As we showed earlier, the solution of the game is straightforward for certain trigger strategies. In a one-shot game, each party gains by making the proper choice, but each gains more by choosing improperly when the other chooses properly. In an indefinitely repeated game, cooperation is again motivated by the discipline that the potential loss of future payoffs imposes. It is a telling example of Smith's remarkable analytic insights that he recognized the incentive issues here, yet did not advocate government intervention. In the light of his understanding of the power of reputational enforcement, as exhibited in *TMS*, this should come as no surprise.

For the most part, though, we confine our application of the Smith game in *WN* to Book V. This Book of *WN*, in our interpretation the first analysis of incentive-compatible state intervention, receives less attention relative to Books I–IV than it deserves – perhaps as a consequence of the rhetorical strategy used by Smith in writing it. His case for incentive-compatible state intervention could not be made effectively without first clearing the way by arguing against mercantilist state intervention. Even that could not be done without a strategy in mind, though, as many of the intended readers in government may have been prejudiced in favor of mercantilist intervention. Smith, a master of rhetoric from his early teaching days, responded to this challenge by using a particular rhetorical strategy: he first emphasized the positive aspects of economic freedom in Books I–III, writing in total opposition to mercantilism without naming mercantilism explicitly as the opponent. Then, after (he hoped) winning the reader's agreement, he attacked the mercantilist system explicitly in Book IV. Finally, in Book V he reached the point where he could argue in favor of government intervention that was truly appropriate. Unfortunately Smith seems to have made his case in Book I–III too persuasive, as he is remembered today primarily for statements made in those Books. We believe his ultimate purpose in writing *WN* is found in Book V, where he makes his case for incentive-compatible state intervention. Book V is rich with implicit games.

Smith identifies in Book V three duties of the sovereign. Two of these duties – the first and second, provision of the public goods defense (*WN*, Book V, Part I) and justice (*WN*, Book V, Part II) – have been analyzed extensively by others both theoretically and experimentally.[10] Public goods provision problems are well known to be isomorph to hawk–dove games; hence the assumptions, tools, and results of game theory apply with force. The third duty of the sovereign is identified by Smith as the provision of public institutions and works:

> The third and last duty of the sovereign or commonwealth is that of erecting and maintaining those public institutions and those public works, which, though they may be in the highest degree advantageous to a great society, are, however, of such a nature, that the profit could never repay the expence to any individual or small number of individuals, and which it therefore cannot be expected that any individual or small number of individuals should erect or maintain. The performance of this duty requires too very different degrees of expence in the different periods of society. After the public institutions and public works necessary for the defence of the society, and for the administration of justice, both of which have already been mentioned, the other works and institutions of this kind are chiefly those for facilitating the commerce of the society, and those for promoting the instruction of the people. (*WN*, p. 681)

One can recognize easily his train of thought: in Book V Smith is concerned first with protecting the people from foreign enemies, second from domestic enemies, and third from other domestic problems which could amount to 'enemies' in a broader sense. One of these problems is an insufficiency of physical capital to facilitate the commerce of the society. The other is an insufficiency of human capital, making necessary instructions of two kinds: 'those for the education of the youth, and those for the instruction of people of all ages' (p. 681).

In Meardon and Ortmann (1995b) we have framed a variety of examples of public goods and externalities from Book V, Part III (street lights, innovation, infant industries, ambassadors, professors, religious sects, and 'supporting the dignity of chief of state') as hawk–dove versions of the Smith game. In these cases, however, the repeated-game cooperative outcome is much less likely to happen. There are many anonymous players, and discerning a cooperator from a defector is difficult, impractical, or impossible – as may be developing a payment scheme whereby people pay up-front and voluntarily. Such are the problems with financing the subsidization of infant industries by voluntary public contribution, for example. Under these circumstances any given player cannot, in a meaningful way, punish defectors with a trigger strategy while playing cooperatively only with other cooperators. Hence the outcome, whether the game is one-shot or indefinitely repeated, is likely to be a Pareto-inefficient one: continuing with the same example, this would mean under- or non-subsidization of the infant industry. Smith believed government could intervene in these cases, with carefully chosen policy, to bring about a more efficient outcome. In this context we have made the case for our claim that Smith was an early theorist of incentive-compatible state intervention.

We have also argued in Meardon and Ortmann (1995b) that our approach allows us to infer what Smith would say, for example, about state intervention regarding present-day telecommunications and issues of computer literacy and quantitative literacy. While answering the question 'What would Smith say if he were alive today?' is outside the scope of the present paper, we can demonstrate application of the Smith game to the third duty of the sovereign in a way that is suggestive of an answer in at least one case. For the remainder of this section, we focus on the analysis of the circumstances that, in Smith's mind, justified the intervention of the state in issues of literacy.

Division of labor externalities
The division of labor is perhaps the most dramatic example Smith provides of a free market's failure to induce optimal outcomes. This might strike many as an outlandish statement; some of the most memorable and well-known passages of *WN*, Book I illustrate how the division of labor is the most important cause of productivity increases. Smith's famous pin factory illustrates nicely the following general principle: 'The division of labour ... so far as it can be introduced, occasions, in every art, a proportionable increase in the productive powers of labour' (*WN*, p. 5). Smith does not change his mind or deny this in Book V. The division of labor does indeed have all the productive power he ascribed to it in Book I, but in addition it has important negative external effects. While most people are educated in the course of their jobs, the division of labor limits their jobs to increasingly specific tasks, and therefore increasingly limits their understandings of the world. Smith does not mince words here:

> In the progress of the division of labour, the employment of the far greater part of those who live by labour, that is, of the great body of the people, comes to be confined to a few very simple operations, frequently to one or two. But the understandings of the greater part of men are necessarily formed by their ordinary employments. The man whose whole life is spent in performing a few simple operations ... becomes as stupid and ignorant as it is possible for a human creature to become. The torpor of his mind renders him, not only incapable of relishing or bearing a part in any rational conversation, but of conceiving any generous, noble, or tender sentiment, and consequently of forming any just

judgment concerning many even of the ordinary duties of private life. (*WN*, pp. 734–5)

We have suggested how in Smith's system people's understanding of the standards of propriety are learned over time (Meardon and Ortmann, 1995a); we also have shown how the standards themselves evolve through social interaction (Ortmann and Meardon, 1995). Each result is highly dependent upon the mind-sets of the people involved. The less educated they are, the longer it will take them to understand and adhere to standards of propriety, and the longer and less adequate will be the evolution of the standards of propriety. 'Propriety' will not be as morally stringent as it was before the division of labor, and people will be less likely to act properly even by the new standards. Smith believed that, if left unaddressed, these external effects of the division of labor could tear the social fabric to pieces. For this reason he thought government *must* address them:

> In some cases the state of the society necessarily places the greater part of individuals in such situations as naturally form in them, without any attention of government, almost all the abilities and virtues which that state requires, or perhaps can admit of. In other cases the state of the society does not place the greater part of individuals in such situations, and some attention of government is necessary in order to prevent the almost entire corruption and degeneracy of the great body of the people. (*WN*, p. 734)

The problem described by Smith is in its underlying structure isomorph to a Bertrand game (essentially a hawk–dove game) with introduction of technology as the decision variable instead of price. As technology progresses, each firm in an industry must decide whether or not to incorporate the new technology into its production process. To do so will allow the firm to gain an edge on its competitor – or at least to keep up, if the competitor chooses to do the same. Introduction of new technology also implies the further division of labor, however, and to that extent it will worsen the 'mental mutilation' of employees. This effect in turn leads to a tearing of the social fabric, a sub-optimal outcome for all parties.

In game-theoretic terms, then, the choices of the firms are to 'do without' new technology or to 'introduce' it. If both firms make the same choice, whatever that choice may be, they end up at the same place they were before: on an even playing field where economic profits are competed away. However, if one firm introduces new technology while the other does not, the firm that introduces it will be at a competitive advantage that translates into greater profits. Though the firm may incur a high fixed cost for the technology, the productivity gains will be such that the firm's average cost will decline and it will be able to undercut its competitor – at the expense of its employees' understanding of the world. The firm that does not introduce the new technology will spare its employees' minds while suffering losses that will ultimately lead to bankruptcy. Given these choices and outcomes, there can be little doubt what firms will choose to do: they will 'introduce' the technology. In strategic form this game may appear as in Figure 4.2.[11]

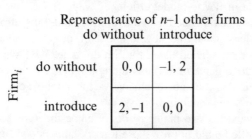

Figure 4.2   The Smith game of division of labor externalities

The game is totally symmetric, hence all firms have the same incentive to introduce the new technology. Once everyone does so economic profits will be zero for every firm, as they were before. Thus the payoffs in the upper left and lower right (diagonal) cells are (0, 0), and the payoffs in the lower left and upper right (off-diagonal) cells are (2, –1) and (–1, –2). The likely outcome of this game, whether repeated or not, is in the lower right corner. The problem is that while firms will be indifferent between the upper left and lower right corners, workers and society may not be. In the upper left corner, the costs of not introducing new technology have to be taken into account; in the lower right corner, the costly impact of the division of labor on the social fabric must be considered.

We argued earlier that Smith, once he was confronted with the empirical evidence that he faced in London, was increasingly concerned about the impact of the division of labor on the mind-sets of workers and consequently on the social fabric. The lengthy passages in Book V that deal with education for the youth and instruction of people of all ages are substantial evidence of his concern.

Our modelling efforts highlight Smith's belief that in many situations government intervention is warranted. However, Smith did not think all methods of intervention are equally appropriate. He was concerned about the incentive compatibility of state intervention. We have belabored this point in more detail in Ortmann and Meardon (1995) and Meardon and Ortmann (1995b). Similar points have been made by Rosenberg (1990) and Rosen (1987).

Discussion and conclusion

We have shown how the Smith game can be applied to model a number of incentive problems in *TMS* and *WN*. We have suggested how Smith used the reputation version of his game in *TMS* to model the acquisition of self-command *given general rules of morality*. (He also used the reputation version of his game in *WN* to model efficiency wages.) We have explained that the current discourse on eductive and evolutive modelling efforts can illuminate Smith's ideas about the development of moral standards, a process which can also be modelled using the Smith game. We have finally argued that the hawk–dove game or variants thereof underlie a variety of problems in *WN*, in particular (but not exclusively) the public good provision and externalities problems found in Book V.

Having analyzed his two major works in game-theoretic terms, we claim that Smith – while he did not use these terms – understood that problems of externalities, leading to undesirable outcomes from society's point of view, pervade the market system. Using the example of division of labor externalities, we have shown that Smith was concerned about the impact of externalities on the social fabric. We have shown elsewhere (Meardon and Ortmann, 1995b) that he was also concerned about state intervention being incentive-compatible.

The pervasive nature of the Smith game bears on two issues: first, it strengthens the case for the authorial unity of *TMS* and *WN*. Second, it leads to a re-evaluation of Smith's importance as an analytical economist. We now turn briefly to these issues.

The Adam Smith problem

In the past, many students of the history of thought viewed *TMS* and *WN* as incongruous or disjointed works. Such a view is the essence of the so-called "Adam Smith problem"'. In its simplest terms, the argument for the Adam Smith problem is normally, 'Smith says in *TMS* that actions are motivated by sympathy, while in *WN* he says that actions are motivated by self-interest.' In their introduction to *TMS*, D.D. Raphael and A.L. Macfie discuss the Adam Smith problem, its origins and its solutions, in greater detail.[12]

The Adam Smith problem seemed to have finally been laid to rest until recently resurrected by Vivienne Brown. In 'Signifying Voices: Reading the "Adam Smith Problem"' she reformulates the problem based on a literary interpretation of what she believes to be the guiding metaphors of *WN* and *TMS*. Brown argues that the moral discourse of *TMS* consistently uses a metaphor of vision, the impartial spectator, to help in understanding moral judgment; on the other hand the economic discourse of *WN* uses a metaphor of invisibility, the invisible hand, to help in understanding the system of natural liberty. In her opinion it follows that: 'Metaphorically, this means that the economic analysis of the system of natural liberty in *WN* is an *amoral discourse*; indeed moral agents are not present in *WN*, neither is the impartial spectator, and neither is a moral discussion of the virtues specific to the marketplace.'

To try here to deconstruct Brown's line of reasoning would force us to wander away from our game-theoretic interpretation. Instead, suffice it to say that by uncovering the pervasive presence of the Smith game throughout his work, we strengthen the case that Raphael and Macfie make. Our assertion that a basic incentive problem underlies both *TMS* and *WN* suggests strongly the congruity of the two.

Smith as an analytical economist

In 'Adam Smith and the Market Mechanism' Salim Rashid first questions whether Smith made relevant contributions to our understanding of the workings of the market mechanism; he argues in addition 'that even the claim that Adam Smith synthesized and improved contemporary understanding of the market is dubious' (p. 149). 'It is not claimed that the eighteenth-century understanding of the market was complete – only that Smith had nothing to add to what already existed. He never went ahead, and frequently stayed behind, the best views of his predecessors' (p. 132). Rashid concludes, 'It is high time that the modern revision, which views Adam Smith as also being an analytical economist, be questioned' (p. 150).

Our assessment of Smith as an early (possibly the first) theorist of incentive-compatible state intervention is sharply at odds with Rashid's view. (Incidentally, Rashid does not mention Book V.) In Rashid's article one finds the following intriguing footnote 3: 'A referee has pointed out that the only criteria used to judge Adam Smith's microeconomics are those of modern neoclassical microeconomics and asked whether such an approach does not unduly distort the insights to be gained from the *Wealth of Nations*. I fully concede that neoclassical microeconomics should not be the only criteria used when judging the overall merits of an economist' (p. 130). While we do not know which alternative approaches the referee had in mind, our approach suggests that the referee's conjecture was right on target.

Finally, a note on Rashid's comments on methodology. We agree that 'theorists must *theorize*' (p. 132); however, whether an economist theorizes or not, or which portions of a book are theoretical and which are not, can be subject to interpretation. Furthermore and more importantly, the structure of a book (or for that matter of an oeuvre) can itself be a reflection of serious theorizing, whether or not it is presented as such explicitly. The wolf in sheep's clothing is still a wolf.

In our view, there can be no doubt that Smith was a major theorist. His vigorous advocacy of economic freedom was a methodological device intended to set the stage for his ultimate purpose: the analysis of incentive-compatible state intervention.

Notes

1. This point is illustrated by Holmstroem and Tirole (1989), Kreps (1990a, 1990b), Barro (1990), and Ostrom (1990).
2. In Meardon and Ortmann (1995a) we have shown how Smith modelled the acquisition of self-command *given general rules of morality* as a game whose structure is identical to endogenous quality or reputation models well known in the game theory literature. In Ortmann and Meardon (1995) we have shown how Smith used the hawk–dove game to model the origin and evolution of general rules of morality.
3. These action choices faced by the Man Today, which may not seem obvious, are justified in Meardon and Ortmann (1995a). In essence, the routine evaluation is a low-cost habit when the Man Yesterday consistently chooses the proper action; it amounts to self-deceit when the Man Yesterday chooses the improper action. The real evaluation is an act of vanity when the Man Yesterday chooses properly – for this reason it is costly in terms of blame-worthiness as well as time and effort; it amounts to atonement, however, when the Man Yesterday chooses improperly.
4. Here we have provided only a very brief exposition of the story underlying the game's equilibria in the one-shot and indefinitely repeated cases under the employment of trigger strategies. A more extensive discussion of the textual justification for the payoffs can be found in Meardon and Ortmann (1995a).
5. Smith stresses that his model of the acquisition of self-command applies to 'The man of real constancy and firmness, the wise and just man who has been thoroughly bred in the great school of self-command, in the bustle and business of the world, ...' (*TMS*, p. 146); Smith cautions that children and people without 'real constancy and firmness' may not be able to gauge the relevant tradeoffs. Smith thus addresses the important issue of the opportunity cost of rational, foresightful behavior. It also bears repeating here that Smith's model of the acquisition of self-command applies to a well-defined class of passions only. In Smith's classification it is the social passions. We discuss Smith's classification and the relation of the social passions to Schelling-type (1978, 1984) passions in Meardon and Ortmann (1995a).
6. See Tullock (1985), Frank (1988), and Binmore (1992).
7. Friedman (1991, 1992a, 1992b), Mailath (1993), and Marimon and McGratten (1993), among others, are concerned with the relation between static and dynamic equilibria. Van Huyck et al. (1994) is concerned with the origin and evolution of conventions.
8. Evensky (1989) makes essentially this argument.
9. In their seminal article on 'The Role of Market Forces in Assuring Contractual Performance', Klein and Leffler (1981, n.5) already gave credit where credit was due.
10. See Davis and Holt (1993), Chap. 6.
11. Note that the game is not of the hawk–dove variety; it is an interesting and instructive variant thereof, though. Note in particular that for the present game it does not matter whether the game is repeated or not.
12. Raphael and Macfie (1982) point out, in one line of reasoning, that *WN* was published after the fourth edition of *TMS*, but before the fifth and sixth editions. Also, the third edition of *WN* (which featured important changes and additions) was published after the fifth edition of *TMS*, and the sixth edition of *TMS* (which, too, featured significant changes and additions) was published after the third edition of *WN*. This 'sandwiching' of the works indicates that during and after the publication of *WN* Smith still had in mind his work in *TMS*.

References

Barro, Robert G. (1990), *Macroeconomic Policy*, Cambridge: Harvard University Press.
Binmore, Ken (1990), *Essays on the Foundations of Game Theory*, Cambridge, Mass.: Basil Blackwell.

Binmore, Ken, *Fun and Games: A Text on Game Theory*, Lexington, Mass.: D.C. Heath.
Brown, Vivienne (1991), 'Signifying Voices: Reading the "Adam Smith Problem"', *Economics and Philosophy*, **7**, pp. 187–220.
Davis, Douglas D. and Charles S. Holt (1993), *Experimental Economics*, Princeton, NJ: Princeton University Press.
Evensky, Jerry (1989), 'The Evolution of Adam Smith's Views on Political Economy', *History of Political Economy*, **21**, pp. 123–45.
Frank, Robert H. (1988), *Passions Within Reason: The Strategic Role of the Emotions*, New York: W.W. Norton.
Friedman, Daniel (1991), 'Evolutionary Games in Economics', *Econometrica*, **59**, pp. 637–66.
Friedman, Daniel (1992a), 'Evolutionary Games: Some Experimental Results', Working Paper, University of California, Santa Cruz.
Friedman, Daniel (1992b), 'Economically Applicable Games', Working Paper, CentER, Tilburg University.
Holmstroem, Bengt R. and Jean Tirole (1989), 'The Theory of the Firm', in *Handbook of Industrial Organization*, vol. 1, ed. R. Schmalensee and R.D. Willig, New York: Elsevier.
Klein, Benjamin and Keith Leffler (1981), 'The Role of Market Forces in Assuring Contractual Performance', *Journal of Political Economy*, **4**, pp. 615–41.
Kreps, David M. (1990a), *Game Theory and Economic Modelling*, New York: Oxford University Press.
Kreps, David M. (1990b), *Microeconomic Theory*, Princeton: Princeton University Press.
Mailath, George J. (1993), 'Introduction: Symposium on Evolutionary Game Theory', *Journal of Economic Theory*, **57**(2), pp. 259–77.
Marimon, Ramon and Ellen McGratten (1993), 'On Adaptive Learning in Strategic Games', *Learning and Rationality in Economics*, Oxford: Basil Blackwell.
Meardon, Stephen J. and Andreas Ortmann (1995a), 'Acquisition of Self-Command in Adam Smith's *Theory of Moral Sentiments:* A Game-theoretic Re-interpretation', Working Paper, Bowdoin College.
Meardon, Stephen J. and Andreas Ortmann (1995b), 'A Game-Theoretic Re-evaluation of Adam Smith's *Wealth of Nations*', Working Paper, Bowdoin College.
Ortmann, Andreas and Stephen J. Meardon (1995), 'Adam Smith on the Origin and Evolution of Moral Sentiments', Working Paper, Bowdoin College.
Ostrom, Elinor (1990), *Governing the Commons: The Evolution of Institutions for Collective Action*, Cambridge: Cambridge University Press.
Raphael, D.D. and A.L. Macfie (1982), 'Introduction' to *The Theory of Moral Sentiments*, Indianapolis: Liberty Classics.
Rashid, Salim (1992), 'Adam Smith and the Market Mechanism', *History of Political Economy*, **24**, pp. 129–52.
Rosen, Sherwin (1987), 'Some Economics of Teaching', *Journal of Labor Economics*, **5**, pp. 561–75.
Rosenberg, Nathan (1990), 'Adam Smith and the Stock of Moral Capital', *History of Political Economy*, **22**, pp. 1–17.
Schelling, Thomas C. (1978), 'Economics, or the Art of Self-Management', *American Economic Review*, **68**, pp. 290–94.
Schelling, Thomas C. (1984), 'Self-Command in Practice, in Policy, and in a Theory of Rational Choice', *AEA Papers and Proceedings*, **74**, pp. 1–11.
Smith, Adam (1982), *The Theory of Moral Sentiments*, ed. D.D. Raphael and A.L. Macfie, Indianapolis: Liberty Classics.
Smith, Adam (1937), *An Inquiry into the Nature and Causes of the Wealth of Nations*, ed. Edwin Cannan. New York: The Modern Library.
Smith, Adam (1983), *Lectures on Rhetoric and Belles Lettres*, ed. J.C. Bryce and A.S. Skinner. Oxford: Clarendon Press.
Tirole, Jean (1989), *The Theory of Industrial Organization*, Cambridge, Mass.: MIT Press.
Tullock, Gordon (1985), 'Adam Smith and the Prisoners' Dilemma', *Quarterly Journal of Economics*, **100** (suppl.), pp. 1073–81.
Van Huyck, John, Raymond Battalio, Sondip Mathur, Andreas Ortmann and Patsy Van Huyck

(1994), 'On the Origin of Convention: Evidence From Symmetric Bargaining Games', *International Journal of Game Theory*, forthcoming.

Appendix: A summary of the basic game-theoretic set-up

To prepare for our comparison of Smith's problem isomorphs, here we lay out, in the starkest manner possible, the tools of game theory we use in this paper.[1]

In its most basic form the 'Smith game' model involves two players with two options each, and will be specified within a two-by-two matrix in so-called strategic form.[2] One player and his two choices will appear along the left vertical axis of the matrix, and the other player and her two choices will appear along the top horizontal axis. The players and their choices will vary according to the particular problem that is being modelled; however, the available strategies can be thought of as strategies of 'cooperating' and 'defecting'.

Each player receives payoffs based upon the choices of both players. Each matrix cell therefore contains a particular set of these payoffs, given first for the Row player, then for the Column player. (In general form, for example, (R_{dc}, C_{dc}) denotes the payoffs to the Row and Column players of the Row player's choice to defect and the Column player's choice to cooperate.) Payoffs can be monetary or non-monetary; for the ease of exposition we assume transferable utility.[3] Furthermore, the players' choices are assumed to be made rationally (in the sense of payoff maximizing), simultaneously, and with common knowledge of the choices and payoffs possible for each player. The generalized strategic game form appears as in Figure 4A.1.

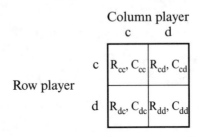

Figure 4A.1   The generalized 'Smith game'

Once we specify the players, their choices, and their payoffs, we will find the Smith game may be either asymmetric or symmetric, depending on the problem modelled.

In its asymmetric version the Smith game is similar to endogenous quality and/or reputation models well known in the game-theory literature. Substituting numerals for the players' payoff variables, a typical parameterization of a reputation game might look as in Figure 4A.2.

Column player
c   d

	c	d
c	1, 1	0, 0
d	2, –1	0, 0

Row player

Figure 4A.2   An asymmetric 'reputation' game

In its symmetric (hawk–dove) version, on the other hand, both players face the same set of payoffs. An example of a typical parameterization looks as in Figure 4A.3.

Column player
c   d

	c	d
c	1, 1	–1, 2
d	2, –1	0, 0

Row player

Figure 4A.3   A symmetric 'prisoner's dilemma' game

Assume for now that both games are played only once. In the reputation game, the Row player is said to have a 'weakly dominant' choice; if he chooses to defect, his payoffs will be at least as good, if not better than if he cooperates. The Column player does not have a weakly dominant choice; but knowing that the Row player does (and that his weakly dominant choice is to defect), she knows she will also be better off choosing to defect. In using this rationale, both players would end up with an outcome that is not Pareto-optimal; nevertheless, when both defect they find themselves in a Nash equilibrium – an outcome where neither has an incentive to change his or her action given the other player's action.

The end result is the same in the hawk–dove game. In this game both players do have a dominant choice: defection. Each player, given either choice of the other player, is better off defecting. This rationale leads them, according to the argument of the model, to mutual defection and the payoff combination in the lower right corner. Just as in the reputation game, the result is not Pareto-optimal; nevertheless, again as in the reputation game, it is a Nash equilibrium.

The outcomes of these games depend crucially on how often they are played, however. Game theory distinguishes between so-called one-shot games (games that are played only once) and two classes of repeated games: finitely repeated games and infinitely repeated games.[4] Because of the similarity of outcomes predicted for one-shot and finitely repeated games, we concentrate only on the one-shot and indefinitely repeated games. As we shall see, if the game is indefinitely repeated, the players may indeed have an incentive to continually play the 'c' strategy.

Consider what the Row player (of either game) must be thinking in an infinitely repeated game: he is still faced with a choice between cooperation and defection, but he now has to assess the payoff gains of cooperation versus defection *over an indefinite period of time*. Assuming both players use a trigger strategy,[5] the Row player knows that if he defects even once, he will never again be able to receive the payoffs of mutual cooperation. Using the payoffs specified in figure 4.1 for example, if the Row player chooses to receive the initially high payoff of 2 units by choosing 'd' while the Column player chooses 'c', he will forever after receive the low payoff of 0 when the Column player catches on in the next round and also plays 'd' (and continues to do so in all future rounds). Each player must weigh not only the payoffs (possibly discounted) in the current round, but the sum of all payoffs in future rounds as well.[6]

The threat of losing the *indefinite* series of payoffs resulting from choosing cooperation may very well prevent the Row player from choosing to defect. In shifting the players' awareness of the game from one-shot to indefinitely repeated, a new Nash equilibrium has emerged: the strategy combination (c, c) has become a Nash equilibrium in the indefinitely repeated game. In the indefinitely repeated game, when both players choose to cooperate, neither would prefer to have taken his alternative strategy option. It is true that in any given round one player could receive a higher payoff by playing 'd' when the other player chooses 'c'; but each knows the other player would react with the trigger strategy, and both players would then be forced into accepting the payoffs of (d, d) for all future rounds. The short-term gains of making a dupe of the other player are a pittance relative to the long-term sacrifice of (c, c) payoffs.

Note that an outside observer watching any single one of the indefinitely repeated encounters might come to the conclusion that the players are 'altruistic' and not out for their self-interest when in fact they are. This important feature, the tradeoff between short-term and long-term payoffs, is the punchline of a rich class of models – which we call summarily the Smith game – representing phenomena as varied as (asymmetrically structured) seller–buyer transactions of goods of adjustable quality or employer–employee relations ('reputation games'), or (symmetrically structured) price competition between oligopolists, attempts of collusion, and problems of externalities and public goods provision ('hawk–dove games'), to mention a few.

Appendix notes

1. For a more comprehensive explanation of these tools see, for example, Kreps (1990a), or Binmore (1992).
2. A given strategic form can correspond to several different extensive form games. Kreps (1990a, pp. 21–5) argues that for certain classes of games the two are different representations of the same game. We shall argue presently that his reasoning applies with force to much of the analysis presented here.
3. Transferable utility requires the relatively strong (if commonly used) assumption of risk neutrality of both players. It also requires that the Von Neumann Morgenstern utility scales have been chosen so that the player's utility $u_i(x) = x$, where i denotes the player. See Binmore (1992), p. 176. While both assumptions are strong, they are standard. For much of our argument they are well justifiable.
4. By a finitely repeated game we mean a game which the players anticipate to end at a particular round. In an indefinitely repeated game the players do not anticipate an end to the game at any particular round, or they may not anticipate an end at all. If the players know the game will stop being repeated at a certain time in the future, standard game theory predicts that each round of the game will be played as if it were a one-shot.
5. Meaning that each will react to a choice of 'd' by the other player by choosing 'd' forever afterwards. In this way the Column player both punishes the Row player, denying him the higher payoffs he could earn from (c, c) or (d, c) outcomes, and protects herself from any additional damage that could be done to her by future (d, c) outcomes. The trigger strategy assumption can be relaxed; it is used here for ease of exposition.
6. Formally, the payoff considerations (shown here for the Row player) are represented by:

$$\sum_{i=1}^{\text{inf.}} (R_{cc}/(1+r)^{i-1}) > R_{dc} + \sum_{i=2}^{\text{inf.}} (R_{dd}/(1+r)^{i-1}). \tag{1}$$

Using the payoffs from Figure 4A.2 these payoff considerations may be specified and reduced to:

$$1 + 1/r > 2. \tag{2}$$

5   A rational reconstruction of Smith's theory of wages

Charles E. Staley

In his well-known commentary on Adam Smith, Mark Blaug (1985) remarks that 'Adam Smith had no consistent theory of wages' (p. 39) and that 'In the space of a half-dozen pages, we meet the wages fund theory, the subsistence theory, the bargaining theory, something like a productivity theory, and even a residual-claimant theory, without any recognition of the fact that these cannot all hold true on the same level of analysis' (p. 44). In my teaching of *The Wealth of Nations* I have routinely taken this approach, but this year when one of my students said that Smith's Book I, Chapter 8 was 'just babble' I considered the matter a little more and proposed the following rational reconstruction to convince the student that Smith made sense after all. It seems to me that the half-dozen theories Blaug mentions do hang together in a coherent whole.[1]

In Book I, Chapter 8 (I.viii in the notation of the Glasgow edition) the concern is with the wage for an average worker; the wage structure account-

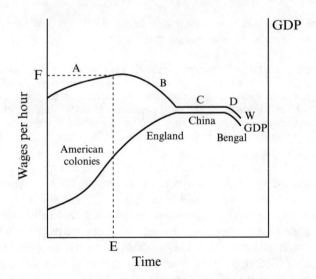

Figure 5.1   Wages and GDP for a hypothetical country over time

ing for the difference in wages between the preacher, the public hangman, and other occupations differing in skill, education, public approbation, and the like are left up to I.x. The top curve in Figure 5.1, which summarizes I.viii.22–6 (the Arabic numerals are the paragraphs in Chapter viii of Book I), shows the history of wages per hour in pounds of a constant purchasing power for a hypothetical country over a long period of time – five hundred to a thousand years or something like that. The names of the countries at various stages on the curve are those with the characteristics which our hypothetical country will take on at the corresponding stages in its history. In Stage A, wages are higher than they are in Stage B, which are higher than they are in Stage C. China, the real-world example of Stage C, is at the subsistence minimum (consuming the garbage thrown overboard from ships and eating dead dogs and cats, in Smith's vivid words), and labour in Stage D is even worse off (Bengal suffers from want, famine, and mortality). The lower curve, measured in units shown on the right vertical axis, shows the progress of 'wealth' (i.e., gross domestic product) over the same stretch of history. Stage A has a rapid growth rate, which is significant because

> It is not the actual greatness of national wealth, but its continual increase, which occasions a rise in the wages of labour. It is not, accordingly, in the richest countries, but in the most thriving, or in those which are growing rich the fastest, that the wages of labour are highest. England is certainly, in the present times, a much richer country than any part of North America. The wages of labour, however are much higher in North America than in any part of England. (I.viii.22)

Accordingly, Stage B is drawn with a higher GDP but less rapid growth. Stage C conforms to the observation that

> Though the wealth of a country should be very great, yet if it has been long stationary, we must not expect to find the wages of labour very high in it. ... China has been long one of the richest, that is, one of the most fertile, best cultivated, most industrious, and most populous countries in the world. It seems, however, to have been long stationary. ... The accounts of all travellers, inconsistent in many other respects, agree in the low wages of labour ... (I.viii.24)

Hence Stage C is drawn with still higher total GDP but no growth. Finally, '... it would be otherwise in a country where the funds destined for the maintenance of labour were sensibly decaying ... Many would not be able to find employment even upon these hard terms, but would either starve, or be driven to seek a subsistence either by begging, or by the perpetration perhaps of the greatest enormities ... This perhaps is nearly the present state of Bengal ...' (I.viii.26). So there is an actual decline of GDP in Stage D. We shall account for these different growth rates shortly and see what the theoretical relation between the two curves is.

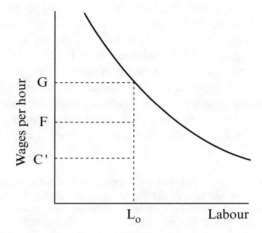

Figure 5.2 The short-run labour market

If we take a vertical slice at any point in the country's history, such as point E, where the wage is at level F, we can put a microscope on the labour market in the short run in Figure 5.2. Wages are indeterminate in the short run, although we can specify a lower and an upper bound. The lower bound, C', is actually the long-run wage in the Chinese stage, C, plus a factor ε which converts the subsistence wage from the physiological minimum of eating half-putrid and stinking dead cats and dogs to the 'lowest (rate) which is consistent with common humanity' (I.viii.16). Evidently in the European civilization which is Smith's primary concern the employer, even though he belongs to the 'order of men, whose interest is never exactly the same with that of the publick, who have generally an interest to deceive and even to oppress the publick, and who accordingly have, upon many occasions, both deceived and oppressed it' (I.xi.10) nevertheless has enough common hu-manity (or, in the language of *The Theory of Moral Sentiments* asks himself what the impartial observer would say and has some positive amount of sympathy) not to push wages all the way down to level C.

The upper bound may be defined in one of two ways. In the beginning of I.viii it is defined as the residual; in the progress from the early and rude state to modern society the landlord's 'rent makes the first deduction from the produce of the labour which is employed upon land' (I.viii.6). Furthermore, the worker is employed by a master whose 'profit makes a second deduction from the produce of the labour which is employed upon land' and 'the produce of almost all other labour is liable to the like deduction of profit' (I.viii.7–8). If the rent and profit shares are well determined the maximum competitive level of wages determined by the residual method should, in a

general equilibrium model, equal the level determined by the partial equilibrium theory of wages. The trouble is that 'Adam Smith had no consistent
theory of ... rents and no theory of profit or pure interest at all' (Blaug, 1985,
p. 39.) But this article is not concerned with Smith's complete theory of
distribution, so we can either ignore the problems with the other shares, or,
alternatively, argue that the residual-claimant theory is barely mentioned
whereas the loanable-funds theory is repeatedly emphasized and used throughout the book. Let us therefore ignore the residual-claimant approach and turn
to loanable funds as the determinant of wage level G, the short-run upper
bound.

> The demand for those who live by wages, it is evident, cannot increase but in
> proportion to the increase of the funds which are destined for the payment of
> wages. These funds are of two kinds; first, the revenue which is over and above
> what is necessary for the maintenance; and secondly, the stock which is over and
> above what is necessary for the employment of their masters.[2] (I.viii.18)

The master spends part of his revenue (i.e., his personal income) on the needs
of his family, and devotes all or part of the rest of it to hiring menial servants.
The independent workman, or master, accumulates more capital than is sufficient to purchase the materials which can be worked up by one man, and
'naturally' employs journeymen with the surplus.[3] In equilibrium the wages
of the menial servants and the journeymen are equal, subject to the wage-
structure considerations of I.x. The maximum wage in the short run is the
total of the wages fund divided by the total amount of labour, adjusted for
time units. (Presumably the wage determined by the wages fund is an annual
wage, which is divided by the typical number of hours worked per year to get
the hourly wage.)

Although the reference to 'the funds which are destined for the employment of labour' implies a fund of money and hence a determination of a
money wage rate, Smith points out that

> The money price of labour is necessarily regulated by two circumstances; the
> demand for labour, and the price of the necessaries and conveniencies of life. The
> demand for labour ... determines the quantity of the necessaries and conveniencies
> of life which must be given to the labourer; and the money price of labour is
> determined by what is requisite for purchasing this quantity. (I.viii.52)

The relation between the real wage and the money wage is in fact determined
by the silver price of corn, which is determined by the international flow of
specie:

> for the money price of corn regulates that of all other home-made commodities. It
> regulates the money price of labour, which must always be such as to enable the

labourer to purchase a quantity of corn sufficient to maintain him and his family either in the liberal, moderate, or scanty manner in which the advancing, stationary or declining circumstances of the society oblige his employers to maintain him. (IV.v.a.11–12)

(See Hollander, 1987, pp. 82–4 for a discussion of this proposition which he says establishes Smith as a genuine model builder.) We can therefore convert the money demand curve for labour into a real demand curve by dividing the money wage by the silver price of corn; since it is the real wage which is important, in the following discussion wages refer to the real wage, and supply and demand are in real terms.

The actual wage at time E is neither C' nor G, but somewhere in between at F. F is the result of the contract set by the bargaining between workmen and masters (I.viii.11–13). Each combines with his peers to force the contract terms to his advantage, but in ordinary circumstances the employers, being fewer in number, find it easier to combine, as well as having the legal advantage that combinations of workmen are prohibited (in 1776) while those of masters are not. Also the masters have the advantage of superior financial resources so that strikes are more easily borne by them than by the workers. The combinations of the masters are generally tacit agreements not to increase wages above the current rate, while the workers' combinations are public, noisy, and tumultuous, usually ending in the intervention of the civil magistrate and the punishment and ruin of the ringleaders. The actual contract, F, is therefore between C' and G, but it is probably closer to G in the 'cheerful' state when GDP is rapidly increasing, but closer to C' as the economy slows down, approaching stage C. F also varies with the state of the harvest: 'Masters of all sorts, therefore, frequently make better bargains with their servants in dear than in cheap years, and find them more humble and dependent in the former than in the latter' (I.viii.48). Dear and cheap years, of course, are defined by the price of wage-goods, specifically, corn. Thus the cost of living influences the wage bargain in a perverse way – workers accept lower wages in drought years in order to get any employment at all, and employers are willing to give higher wages in years of 'sudden and extraordinary plenty' (I.viii.52). (The editors of the Glasgow edition of *The Wealth of Nations*, who have the benefit of B.R. Mitchell's *Abstract of British Historical Statistics*, note that Smith overstates his case. *Wealth of Nations*, p. 102.)

The 'something like a productivity theory' which Blaug mentions as one of the grab-bag of theories which Smith presented in the beginning of the chapter is actually a continuation of I.vi.1, the 'early and rude state of society which precedes both the accumulation of stock and the appropriation of land', when 'the proportion between the quantities of labour necessary for acquiring different objects seems to be the only circumstance which can afford any rule for exchanging them for one another'. In this state, Smith notices at the beginning of I.viii, the wages of labour would have been augmented with any improved productivity from the division of labour. There would have been no one with whom to share the improved output so the return of labour would rise. But this state of things ends when other factors of production come on the scene, which is 'long before the most considerable improvements were made in the productive powers of labour, and it would be to no purpose to trace farther what might have been its effects upon the recompence or wages of labour' (I.viii.5). Economics would have to wait for the marginal productivity theory of wages, and we do not need to try to enter it in Figure 5.2.

So far we have determined point F as one point on the short-run demand curve for labour. Determining the complete short-run demand curve requires a little more analysis. If Smith had opted for the subsistence theory of wages the demand curve would have been a horizontal line; if he had left it at the wages fund theory the demand curve would have been a unit-elastic curve whose equation is

$$W = WF/L \tag{1}$$

(where W = wage/hour, WF = Wages Fund, and L = man-hours of labour). If the employers by their superior bargaining power are able to reduce wages by the fraction λ, the demand equation becomes

$$W = WF\,(1 - \lambda)/L. \tag{2}$$

The employer's revenue this period is increased by λWF. Adopting a period analysis in which this period's revenue affects next period's decisions, what effect does the additional revenue λWF_1 have on WF_2? Some of the additional revenue goes directly into hiring menial servants, as discussed above. But hiring menial servants does not increase next year's wages fund; the wages fund, in the classical real theory of capital, is a stock of wages goods, and menial labour is unproductive labour. 'A man grows rich by employing a multitude of manufacturers: He grows poor, by maintaining a multitude of menial servants ... the labour of the manufacturer fixes and realizes itself in some particular subject or vendible commodity, which lasts for some time at least after that labour is past' (II.iii.1).

Some of the additional revenue is saved, but we know that Smith believed in Say's Law so that the additional saving goes directly into capital formation, including an increase in the wages fund. 'Capitals are increased by parsimony, and diminished by prodigality and misconduct' (II.iii.14). 'What is annually saved is as regularly consumed as what is annually spent, and nearly in the same time too, but by a different set of people ... by labourers, manufacturers, and artificers' (II.iii.18).

But some of the additional revenue is spent on luxury goods, and this does not affect the demand for labour. As John Stuart Mill explained with reference to the wages-fund model,

> Demand for commodities is not demand for labour. The demand for commodities determines in what particular branch of production the labour and capital shall be employed; it determines the *direction* of the labour; but not the more or less of the labour itself, or of the maintenance or payment of the labour. These depend on the amount of the capital, or other funds directly devoted to the sustenance and remuneration of labour.[4]

So two of the employer's three options – hiring menial servants or buying consumer goods – do not affect the wages fund, but the third option – saving – increases it next period above the level shown by L_0G in Figure 5.2.

To analyse the exact effects of the employer's extracting λWF_1 and then saving some of what we might term his exploitative income, assume that in Stage A the wages fund grows each year by γ per cent, so that without any exploitation

$$WF_2 = WF_1 (1 + \gamma). \tag{3}$$

With exploitation, the gross wages fund in period 2 grows to

$$WF_2 = WF_1 (1 + \gamma) + WF_1 (\lambda) MPS = WF_1 \{(1 + \lambda) + \gamma MPS\}, \tag{4}$$

where *MPS* is the employers' marginal propensity to save. Therefore the gross wages fund grows faster (i.e., shifts more to the right) when there is bargaining power for the employer than where there is not. But the employee gets only $1 - \lambda$ of the WF_2 shown in equation (4), and

$$(1 - \lambda) WF_2 = [WF_1\{(1 + \gamma) + \lambda MPS\}] (1 - \lambda) \tag{5}$$

Under bargaining as compared to the no-bargaining case the worker gains

$$WF_1 MPS (1 - \lambda), \tag{6}$$

and loses

$$\lambda WF_1 (1 + \gamma). \tag{7}$$

The net gain or loss is the sum of (6) and (7), which is

$$\lambda WF_1[MPS(1 - \lambda) - (1 + \gamma)]. \tag{8}$$

Since *MPS* and $(1 - \lambda)$ are both between 0 and 1, while $(1 + \gamma)$ is greater than 1 in stages A and B but equal to 1 in stage C, (8) is negative. Therefore the worker loses under bargaining, even though the gross wages fund increases. The net demand curve for labour shifts to the right by a smaller amount under exploitation than it does when the employer has no bargaining power. But this does not eliminate the grand stages of history shown in Figure 5.1, although the points of transition from one stage to another are affected. The decline of wages as the economy moves from Stage A to Stage B occurs earlier in history under bargaining, because in the race between increases in demand and increases in supply the reduced growth of demand under bargaining allows supply changes to get ahead of demand sooner than they otherwise would.

At the conclusion of the previous paragraph we shifted the discussion from the short run to the long run. The short-run demand curves in Figure 5.3 are the wages fund net of the amounts extracted from labour by the bargaining power of the employer.[5] Using a period analysis, in period 1 the wage is W_1. In period 2 the wages fund increases and before the labour force has time to expand the wage will rise to W_2 (the wage is the F of Figure 5.2, the result of the bargaining carried out between employer and worker). Even though the size of the labour force is constant, the higher wage calls forth more labour. 'Where wages are high, accordingly, we shall always find the workmen more

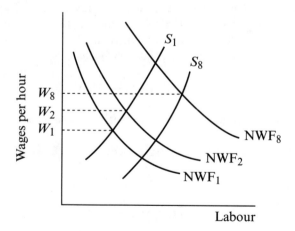

Figure 5.3   Short-run demand and supply curves in Stage A

active, diligent, and expeditious than where they are low; in England, for example, than in Scotland; in the neighbourhood of great towns than in remote country places' (I.viii.44). The wages-fund curve continues to shift to the right, and after a period of years long enough for the children born in year 1 to enter the labour force, the supply curve shifts to the right also. (In Smith's day that might have been eight years, before child-labour laws; also, once the process is started, there will be an annual shift to the right in the labour-supply curve.) But the growth of capital is more rapid than the growth of labour, so the wage increases from W_1 to W_8.

But eventually the economy moves from Stage A to Stage B and the wage rate starts to fall. This requires that the annual shift in the wages fund becomes less than the annual rightward shift of the labour supply, as in Figure 5.4.

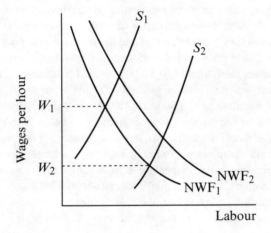

Figure 5.4 Supply and demand shifts in Stage B

(The shift parameter γ is less in Stage B than in Stage A, and is equal to zero in Stage C, becoming negative in Stage D.) One reason why the rate of growth of the wages fund decreases is that the returns to investment fall:

> The increase of stock, which raises wages, tends to lower profit. When the stocks of many rich merchants are turned into the same trade, their mutual competition naturally tends to lower its profit; and when there is a like increase of stock in all the different trades carried on in the same society, the same competition must produce the same effect in them all. (I.ix.2)

Another reason given by Smith, which is not persuasive,[6] is that of II.v: there is a hierarchy of investment, which in order of productivity is agriculture, manufacturing, wholesaling, and retailing; over the course of time the most productive outlets, agriculture and manufacturing, are filled up (unless unwise policy distorts the pattern of investment) and subsequent investment in wholesaling and retailing will yield less. Not only does this slow-down in the productivity of capital begin to lower wages; it also lowers the rate of growth of GDP in Figure 5.1.

As wages start to decline, the rate of growth of labour supply increases. Children are inferior goods. 'Poverty, though it no doubt discourages, does not always prevent marriage. It seems even to be favourable to generation' (I.viii.37). 'It is the sober and industrious poor who generally bring up the most numerous families, and who principally supply the demand for useful labour' (V.ii.k.7). On the other hand, 'a pampered fine lady is often incapable of bearing any (children), and is generally exhausted by two or three ... Luxury in the fair sex, while it enflames perhaps the passion for enjoyment, seems always to weaken and frequently to destroy altogether, the powers of generation'[7] (I.viii.37). The downward trend of wages caused by the slowdown of the rate of increase of labour demand and the increase in the rate of growth of labour supply continues until the stationary state, Stage C, is reached (or even worse, the unfortunate Stage D). Stage C would be characterized by a constant GDP and hence no change in capital formation or the wages fund, and by a constant population with wages at the physiological subsistence level.

The purpose of the paper was to examine whether it is true that Smith's listing of wage theories was inconsistent, or 'cannot all be true on the same level of analysis'. I am not sure what is meant by the level of analysis – short-run *vs* long-run, or partial *vs* general equilibrium, or rigorous economics *vs* intuitive economics. But a rational reconstruction of the sort outlined here shows that Smith's comments can be woven into a consistent theory stretching from the very short run to the entire life-span of the nation.[8]

Notes

1. Hollander (1987), p. 77, cites an additional wage theory, the 'imputation' theory, on the basis of V.iii.76. In that passage Smith claims that a reduction in taxes on wage goods would enable workers to live more cheaply and hence reduce the cost of goods. The result would be an increase in the demand for goods and hence in the demand for labour; thus the demand for labour is a function of the demand for the final product. Since this is a comment in passing and is not used by Smith in his general discussion of wages, it seems inappropriate to regard it as a significant aspect of Smith's wage theory.
2. Hollander (1987), p. 76, refers to the wages-fund approach of aggregative analysis in Smith. In this paper the aggregative labour demand fund is regarded as the summation of the wages funds accumulated by individual employers.
3. The chapter on productive and unproductive labour, II.iii, has a similar formulation: 'That part of the annual produce ... which replaces a capital, never is immediately employed to maintain any but productive hands. ... That which is immediately destined for constituting a revenue either as profit or as rent, may maintain indifferently either productive or unproductive hands' (II.iii.5). The unproductive labour is the menial servant and the productive labour is the journeyman of I.viii.

4. Mill (I.v.9) (Ashley edition, p. 79). See Blaug (1985), pp. 184–5, for a mathematical proof that an increase in spending on luxury goods and personal labour services reduces the wages fund.
5. Figure 5.3 is a modification of Blaug (1985), Figure 2–3, p. 44.
6. See Stigler (1976).
7. Perhaps Smith made this sociological observation during his trip to France as tutor of the Duke of Buccleuch.
8. Caravale (1988) argues that in Smith the natural wage is given by institutional factors such as the difference in bargaining power and the customary and cultural factors determining the 'subsistence level' which were analysed above. His objection to such formulations as in the present paper is that supply and demand forces should not be taken as supply and demand functions but rather as elements exerting upwards and downwards pressure around the exogenous natural wage. The thrust of my paper is that the natural (i.e., long-run) wage is not exogenous but is a function of the stage of the nation's history. This stage is determined by the rate of capital accumulation which depends on the rate of return and its decline as capital grows. The proposition is true even though 'Smith's rationale is riddled with difficulties' (Hollander, 1987, p. 162). I am grateful to Professor Caravale for helpful comments on this paper at the History of Economics Conference, June, 1993.

References

Blaug, Mark (1985), *Economic Theory in Retrospect*, fourth ed., Cambridge: Cambridge University Press.
Caravale, Giovanni (1988), 'The Notion of Natural Wage and Its Role in Classical Economics', *Rivista Internazionale di Scienze Economische e Commerciali*, **XXXV**, pp. 599–624.
Hollander, Samuel (1987), *Classical Economics*, Oxford: Basil Blackwell.
Mill, John Stuart (1848 [1909]), *Principles of Political Economy*, ed. W.J. Ashley, London: Longman, Green.
Smith, Adam (1776 [1976]), *An Inquiry into the Nature and Causes of the Wealth of Nations*, Glasgow edition, ed. Campbell, Skinner and Todd, Oxford: Oxford University Press.
Stigler, George (1976), 'The Successes and Failures of Professor Smith', *Journal of Political Economy*, **84**, pp. 1199–213.

6 Institutionalist supports in the classical economics of J.S. Mill

Hans E. Jensen[1]

Introduction

As an economist working in the tradition of classical political economy, John Stuart Mill endeavoured to formulate a 'general theory of the economic progress of society'. He added, however, that it 'is only in the backward countries of the world that increased production is still an important object: in those most advanced', such as Great Britain, 'what is economically needed is a better distribution' (*CW*, 3, pp. 752, 755).[2] And, said he, the 'Distribution of wealth', in the sense of real income, 'is a matter of institutions solely' (*CW*, 3, p. 199). This distribution was so unfavourable to the labouring classes that they were impoverished to such an extent that '[f]irst among existing social evils may be mentioned the evil of Poverty' (*CW*, 5, p. 712). Hence, said Mill,

> I must repeat my conviction, that the industrial economy which divides society absolutely into two portions, the payers of wages and the receivers of them, the first counted by the thousands and the last by the millions, is neither *fit for*, nor *capable of*, indefinite duration. (*CW*, 3, p. 896); emphasis added)

Not all institutions wee inherently pernicious, however. Although crippled at the time that Mill was writing, some institutions harboured the potentialities for an improvement of the conditions of the presently poor. If their growth were encouraged, some of these institutions would be capable of guiding the application of the 'extensions of our knowledge' in such a manner that increases would occur in the 'productiveness of labour' (*CW*, 2, p. 199). Other beneficial institutions would have the capacity of effecting 'a better distribution' of the resultant 'increase of aggregate wealth' so that the 'poor might grow rich ... [because] the means of enjoyable existence [would] be more and more largely diffused' (*CW*, 3, p. 709).

Mill's concern with the existing vicious institutions and with the potentially virtuous institutions of the future provided me with an agenda for the present study. In the first place, I shall endeavour to explain how Mill conceived of institutions. Second, I shall attempt to identify those institutions that he viewed as being principally responsible for the 'suffering of the poor' (*CW*, 26, p. 278). Third, I shall strive to explain the nature of those proposals for reform that Mill put forth with a view to eliminating poverty through empowerment of the virtuous institutions.

Mill on institutions: some concepts

Unlike some twentieth-century institutionalists with a Veblenian bent,[3] Mill's concept of institutions was cast in a dualistic mould. To him, each of a number of important institutions was both a 'structural category' and 'a functional category' (Ayres, 1952, p. 42).

Institutions as structural categories

When he viewed institutions as structures, or as 'sub-parts' of society (Ayres, 1952, p. 42), Mill found that the following institutions were relevant for his inquiry into the causes, consequences and remedies of poverty: the 'government', social 'classes', and business 'establishments' that were organized as sole proprietorships 'carried on by scattered individuals', as 'partnerships', and as 'joint stock companies' (*CW*, 2, pp. 13, 19, 20; 3, p. 901; and 2, p. 135). In terms of market power, business structures in the Millian world ranged all the way from firms that engaged in 'unimpeded competition' with each other to 'monopolies' (*CW*, 2, p. 243; and 3, p. 928). Other institutional structures were workers' 'combinations to raise wages', workers' 'cooperative societies', elementary 'schools', 'High School[s]', and 'Universities' (*CW*, 3, pp. 932, 793; 4, p. 376; and 21, pp. 220, 221).

Mill paid attention to institutions as structures because it was as structures that most 'social institutions' had a direct, but *functional*, impact upon the lives of the multitudes (*CW*, 1, p. 384).

Institutions as functional categories

According to Mill, therefore, the power and roles of institutions as sub-parts of society were rooted in the very same institutions' functional and behavioural aspects. Moreover, there were some very important institutions that lacked structure altogether. Hence these institutions were purely functional in nature. As far as Mill was concerned, the most important *economic* institution, 'property', was found in this category. By Mill's time, the institution of property had become vested with a 'sacredness' that was reserved normally for religious symbols. It was around this 'primary and fundamental [economic] institution' that Mill located some of the above-mentioned structures as satellite institutions that, together with property itself, shaped the lives of human beings (*CW*, 28, p. 256; and 2, p. 200).

Institutions are capable of shaping lives because they are the locus of behaviours that have been customized, so to speak. As Mill put it, behavioural patterns 'pertain to customary circumstances, and customary characters'. He identified two kinds of customs, however. One set is static and

change-resisting in that these customs foster a type of institutionalized behaviour that preserves and conserves the *status quo*. '[C]onformity is the first
thing thought of' so that a person's principal 'faculty' becomes an 'ape-like
one of imitation'. Consequently, the 'despotism of [static] custom is every-
where the standing hindrance to human advancement' (*CW*, 18, pp. 262, 265,
272).

Fortunately, said Mill, there is another kind of customs, namely customs
that have been 'cultivated in ... [a] direction' that leads to an 'ultimate
improvement' of the human character and the human condition (*CW*, 10,
p. 230; and 1, p. 239).

But why is it that 'habits can be ... moulded' into institutionalized behaviour either by past-binding and static customs or by forward-looking and
progressive customs? Because of the 'astonishing pliability' of that which
Mill called 'human character' (*CW*, 18, p. 145; and 10, p. 293).

Human nature and character
Mill distinguished between 'human nature' and human character. By human
nature, he understood 'those parts of our mental and moral constitution
which are ... innate'. Thus he viewed human nature as an '*ensemble*' of
'instincts' among which 'selfishness' and 'sympathy' are pre-eminent. Significantly, Mill contrasted the innate propensities of the human being with
'those which are acquired' (*CW*, 2, p. 200; and 10, pp. 399, 374, 393, 394). It
was to the latter traits that he affixed the label human character. As he put it, a
'person whose desires and impulses are his own – are the expression of his
own nature, as it has been developed and *modified* by his own culture – is
said to have a *character*' (*CW*, 18, p. 264; emphasis added). Thus as pointed
out by Janice Carlisle, '*Character* for Mill is, most often, a specifically
human version of his definition of *nature*, and it signifies a thoroughly condi-
tioned phenomenon' (Carlisle, 1991, p. 1). It is no wonder, therefore, that
human character plays a much more important role in Mill's account of
human behaviour than does human nature. He even went so far as to argue
that 'the truth is that there is hardly a single point ... belonging to human
character, which is not decidedly repugnant to the untutored feelings of
human nature'. In short, the elements of character are 'evidently not instinc-
tive, but a triumph over instinct' (*CW*, 10, pp. 393, 394).

When he endeavoured to explain how the culturally nurtured character of
the human being functions, Mill employed a 'Psychological Theory' of 'Experience and Association' (*CW*, 9, p. 178; and 1, p. 269) that is a nearly
perfect echo of his father's, James Mill's, psychological associationism (J.
Mill, 1967).

The younger Mill postulated that an individual's 'belief in an external
world is not intuitive, but an acquired product'. He based this assertion on the

'following psychological truths': 'first, that the human mind is capable of Expectation' and of 'Memory' and, second, that experience is gained through the operation of the 'laws of Association of Ideas' (*CW*, 9, pp. 177; 31, p. 170).

The essence of the first truth is that 'after having had actual sensations, we are capable of forming the conception of Possible sensations; sensations which we are not feeling at the present moment, but which we ... should feel if certain conditions were present, the nature of which conditions we have, in many cases, learnt by experience' (*CW*, 9, p. 177). Something is left, however, after a sensation ceases. Following his father (J. Mill, 1967, vol. 1, p. 52), Mill viewed this trace as a copy of the sensation in question, a copy that both of the Mills called 'idea': we 'have sensations, and we have copies of these sensations, called ideas of them'. But some ideas may not be copies of personally felt sensations. 'I have an idea of Hamlet, and of Falstaff', said Mill; 'combinations which, though made up of ideas of sensation, never existed at all in the world of sense; they never were anything more than ideas in my mind'. Having had these 'ideas presented to me through the words of Shakespeare, I have formed what is properly an idea ... of an idea in Shakespeare's mind; and I may communicate my idea to others, whose idea will then be an idea of an idea in my mind' (*CW*, 31, pp. 109, 110).

According to the laws of the association of ideas, '[s]imilar phaenomena tend to be thought of together' as do phenomena 'which have either been experienced or conceived in close contiguity to one another'. And when 'two phaenomena have been very often experienced in conjunction ... there is produced between them ... [an] Inseparable ... Association', by which Mill meant that it is 'impossible for ... [an individual] to think the one thing disjoined from the other' (*CW*, 9, pp. 177, 178).

A person's 'conception of the world ... consists, in only a small proportion, of present sensations'. It is formed largely by

> a countless variety of possibilities of sensation: namely the whole of those which past observation tells me that I could, under any supposable circumstances, experience at this moment, together with an indefinite and illimitable multitude of others which though I do not know that I could, yet it is possible that I might, experience in circumstances not known to me. (*CW*, 9, p. 179)

Although the limitless possibilities are shrouded in the mist of the individual's ignorance about the conditions in which they might be experienced, they are still in the realm of possibility: 'they are potentially present, ready to be realized by association if the opportunity permits. If they are not actually present to the mind, their *possibility* is actually present' (Wilson, 1990, p. 170). Moreover, in contradistinction to one's 'present sensations', which are 'fugitive', the possibilities 'are permanent'. And, Mill added, the 'permanent possibilities are common to us and to our fellow-creatures: the actual sensations are not'. Consequently, the permanent possibilities' 'groundwork in sensation is forgotten' in most cases (*CW*, pp. 180, 182). Prominent among such cases are those in which individuals, or groups of individuals, receive ideas that have been developed by other individuals or groups. It is this notion of the possibility of interpersonal, and intergroup, transfers of ideas about the world, and about one's position therein, that undergirds Mill's institutionalist analysis and his resultant recommendations for institutional reform. As will be discussed below, Mill was of the opinion that reforms should be designed to eliminate 'those differences, whether between individuals or sexes' that are 'produced by differences in circumstances' (*CW*, 1, p. 270).

Mill on institutions: behaviour and categorical aspects

In his analysis of institutions, Mill endeavoured to find an answer to the following twofold question: why do institutions behave as they do, and, if their behaviour is socially undesirable, how can it be modified through institutional reforms? He maintained that the beginning of an answer could be found only by means of analyses that are informed by history and guided by 'social philosophy' (*CW*, 2, p. 201).

In what may be viewed as his point of departure for such an analysis, Mill provided an illustration of how a change in the social milieu may cause a recustomization of behaviour because new experiences foster new sensations that are copied as new ideas that become institutionalized.

> We may suppose [said Mill] ... a body of colonists, occupying for the first time an uninhabited country; bringing nothing with them but what belonged to them in common, ... [They were] required, therefore, to choose whether they would conduct the work of production on the principle of individual property, or on some system of common ownership and collective agency. If private property were adopted, we must presume that it would be accompanied by none of the initial inequalities and injustices which obstruct the beneficial operation of the principle in old societies. (*CW*, 2, p. 201)

Thus it appears that Mill anticipated Clarence E. Ayres's Pirenneesque frontier thesis according to which frontier life promotes unorthodox ways of doing things.[4] It was Mill's main concern, however, to discover how dynamic and change-promoting customs, similar in quality to those bred on the frontier, might be substituted for static and change-resisting customs in a settled and relatively developed country, such as Great Britain of his time. This required that an inquiry be made into the reasons that the poor accepted obediently their station in life.

Pernicious institutions as causes of poverty and injustice
In Mill's opinion, it was an assemblage of four institutions that caused the
'condition of [large] numbers ... in England ... [to be] more wretched than
that of most tribes of savages who are known to us'. That was so, he argued,
because three of the four groups of institutions were so powerful that they
had been successful in creating a situation in which the 'very idea of distributive justice ... is ... so manifestly chimerical as to be relegated to the regions
of romance' (*CW*, 5, pp. 713, 714). The fourth class of institutions was so
deprived of power that those whose behaviour was associated therewith
accepted without objection a state of poverty that had been bestowed upon
them by the income-distorting activities of the other three sets of institutions.
The economically powerful classes of institutions were the state, educational
institutions, and the institution of private enterprise. The powerless group
consisted of the numerous households of the institution of the working-class
family.

The state was a super-institution that consisted of Parliament, Cabinet, and
the Judiciary. In Mill's view, it was a super-institution in the sense that it
served as the guardian of 'that primary and fundamental [*economic*] institution [of property], on which ... the economical arrangements of society have
always rested'. In exercising its function as a protector of property, the state
had 'purposefully fostered inequalities, and prevented all from starting fair in
the race'. In full cooperation with administrators and justices in the other
branches of the state, the makers of 'legislation' had taken 'much pains ... to
aggravate the inequality of chances arising from the natural working of the
principle' of private property (*CW*, 2, pp. 200, 207, 208). The consequences
of the working of this principle, Mill described thus:

> [T]he institution of private property necessarily carried with it as a consequence,
> that the produce of labour should be apportioned as we now see it, almost in an
> inverse ratio to the labour – the largest portions to those who have never worked
> at all, the next largest to those whose work is almost nominal, and so on in a
> descending scale, the remuneration dwindling as the work grows harder and more
> disagreeable, until the most fatiguing and exhausting bodily labour cannot count
> with certainty on being able to earn even the necessaries of life. (*CW*, 2, p. 207)

The powers that be were fully aware, however, that a continuation of the
existing distribution of property, wealth, and income depended on the fulfilment of two conditions: first, the provision of a continuous supply of decision
makers for service in public and private agencies who possessed a politically
correct *Weltanschauung* and, second, an unceasing willingness on the part of
the masses to accept unquestionably their station in life. In Mill's opinion,
the responsibility for assuring that these objectives be achieved had been
delegated by the state to educational institutions.

Education was in a state of serious underdevelopment in Mill's Britain. In his words, 'all classes, from the highest to the lowest, are wretchedly ill-taught'. As far as the universities and secondary schools 'for the higher and middle classes' were concerned, there were 'enough of them, and they ha[d] funds enough to give a good education'. Nevertheless, said Mill, '[w]e are, thanks to our Church and our Universities, a most unlearned nation. Those 'venerable institutions' have nearly rooted out learning from among us'. 'Why is this?' Mill asked. And he answered: as far as the universities are concerned, '[b]ecause the teachers are unfit for their work, or at all events do not do it' (*CW*, 28, p. 322; 1, p. 529). The shortcomings of the faculties were that they failed to encourage their students to familiarize themselves with ideas that were reflections, or copies, of those sensations that were experienced recently by scholars in the natural and cultural sciences. Instead, the faculties inculcated their students with opinions that were copies of forgotten sensations that were felt in bygone ages. Consequently, higher education 'has remained far behind ... the actual state of the human mind ... and instead of going hand in hand with civilisation has not even condescended to follow'. The fatal flaw in higher education was that the 'Universities may be regarded for all practical purposes as ecclesiastical establishments, and education [therein] ... may be considered as being in the hands of the clergy'. And unfortunately, 'the business for which they are paid, is not to make the human mind advance but ... to keep it where it is' (*CW*, 26, pp. 348, 348–9).

The importance of all this was that the ecclesiastical hierarchy, which had spread its tentacles into the universities, was 'a hierarchy connected with the ruling powers in the state' from which its members received their 'emoluments'. Hence it had become 'the interest of its members to uphold certain political ... opinions, and to uphold them whether they are right or wrong' (*CW*, 26, p. 350). Thus for all practical purposes, the universities served the state's interest in preserving the existing property relations.

'The elementary schools for the children of the working classes, are still worse' than the universities and the 'grammar schools'. Although there were not sufficient schools for the children of the poor, the real problem was that the existing schools did not provide true education. '[M]ind must be taught by mind' and there was a shortage of minds capable of teaching. 'Even if we were to think with the vulgar', said Mill, 'that any one who knows a thing can teach it – even so the bulk of the existing schoolmasters could teach nothing, for they know nothing; no *thing*, no *words* even'. Consequently, 'the children do not at present even learn to read'. And, of course, there was '[n]o attempt ... to communicate ideas, or to call forth the mental faculties' of pupils (*CW*, 6, pp. 199–200).

Those few qualified teachers who attempted to teach were frustrated. 'A teacher whose heart is in the work, and who attempts any enlargement of the instruction, often finds his greatest obstacle in fears of patrons and managers lest the poor should be "over-educated"' (*CW*, 4, p. 377). Mill was referring to the managers of some charitable organizations who had financed the construction of school buildings but who were opposed to 'a state provision ... for education' because it was their 'constant alarm' that 'too much, should be taught' in elementary schools (*CW*, 21, p. 65). This alarm was shared by those politically powerful groups that, in and out of government, promoted the state's policies of malignant neglect of elementary education. As a result of this successful effort, the 'want of the mind, the want of being wiser and better ... [was] unfelt' on the part of the working poor (*CW*, 4, p. 213). Thus being both ignorant and blissfully unaware of their own ignorance, the uneducated masses were gullible and accepted uncritically the justification for, and celebration of, the existing order as they were exhorted to do by the institutions of state, church and education.

Although the principal purpose of the educational institutions was to ensure a continuous acceptance of the institution of private property on the part of the populace, another specialized institution was needed to bring about that 'apportionment' of income 'in an inverse ratio to ... labour' that was required if the institution of private property were to bestow its blessings upon those who laid claim to it (*CW*, 2, p. 207). Through its policy of *laissez-faire*, the state delegated this allocating function to the institution of private enterprise.

Private enterprises and markets were the institutions that regulated the activities of all economically active persons in the capitalist order that Mill analysed. It was an order in which the accumulation of capital was propelled by 'new technical inventions' that caused a continuous expansion of the 'fund from which savings can be made'. According to Mill, it was the institutional arrangements in the market for labour that ensured that the bulk of this surplus ended up as 'returns to the capitalist' rather than being funnelled into the 'wages fund' that sustained the worker (*CW*, 2, pp. 189, 160, 161, 337). He described these arrangements thus.

Wages 'depend mainly upon the demand and supply of labour'. Unfortunately, 'the existing habits' of the working classes, in conjunction with the capitalists' habitual search for maximum 'profits', ensured that wages tended to gravitate toward that which the workers viewed as a minimum subsistence rate. The workers' habits in question were those that deprived them of any 'inducements not to marry'. Consequently, the members of the working classes exercised hardly any 'control ... over the animal power of multiplication' (*CW*, 2, pp. 337, 188, 402, 347, 354).

At any given point in time, accumulation, and the resultant increase in the demand for labour, tended to engender an increase in wages rates that made marriage affordable for more young people than hitherto. Because of the workers' sexual habits, this caused a subsequent swelling of the population and an expansion of the supply of labour. In spite of temporary deviations therefrom, the result was the establishment of a long-run 'rate of wages, [that is] either the lowest on which the people can, or the lowest on which they will consent, to live'. And 'though they would gladly have more, [they] will live on that (as the fact proves) rather than restrain the instinct of multiplication' (*CW*, 2, p. 361).

There was a second set of forces in the economy that contributed to the misery of the working classes. These were forces in the market for commodities that moulded business behaviour in such a manner that 'competition either [was] not taking place at all, or producing its effect in quite a different manner from that which is ordinarily assumed to be natural to it' (*CW*, 2, p. 239).

In the first place, it is customary among retailers to sell 'the same article at different prices to different customers: and, as a general rule, each retailer adapts his scale of prices to the class of customers whom he expects'. Hence the 'price paid by the actual consumer, seems to feel very …imperfectly the effect of competition'. On the whole, the ability of the retailers to practise some degree of price administration results in a system which, 'instead of lowering prices, merely divides the gains of the high price among a greater number of dealers' (*CW*, 2, pp. 242, 243). Second, cartels may be formed. They flourish in particular, but not exclusively, among 'railways' and 'gas and water' companies where 'competitors are so few, [that] they always end by agreeing not to compete. They may run a race of cheapness to ruin a new candidate, but as soon as he has established his footing they come to terms with him' (*CW*, 2, pp. 142, 141). Finally, modern technology has brought into existence 'many cases in which production is made much more effective by being conducted on a large scale'. In other words, 'large manufactories' are the result of the 'introduction of processes requiring expensive machinery. Expensive machinery supposes a large capital', however. The problem of financing was solved 'by the practice of forming a large capital by the combination of many small contributions; or, in other words, by the formation of joint stock companies'. This technology-driven modification of the institution of property spawned another alteration of that institution, namely a separation of ownership from control: 'shareholders' own and 'hired servants' control. In Mill's words, the 'administration of a joint stock association is … administered by hired servants'. Although they are 'supposed to superintend the management', the members of the 'board of directors' do not do so because they divide 'their time with many other occupations'. Hence the business is 'the principal concern of no one except those who are hired to carry it out' (*CW*, 2, pp. 131, 133, 135, 137).

Because of the advantage of large-scale operations, there 'is a perpetual growth not only of large manufacturing establishments, but also … of shops and warehouses for conducting retail business on a large scale'. And Mill emphasized that because of their superior efficiency, the large corporate firms 'are almost always able to undersell the smaller tradesmen'. Consequently, 'business of all kinds [is being thrown] more and more into the hands of large ... joint-stock companies' (*CW*, 2, p. 141; and 18, p. 136).[5]

Given the tendency of money wages to gravitate toward a minimum subsistence rate, private price administration made it increasingly onerous for the working classes to bear the burden of the maldistribution of nominal income.

The working-class family was therefore immersed in poverty to such an extent that the 'condition of [large] numbers' of workers was, as mentioned above, 'more wretched than that of most tribes who are known to us'. Because of their poverty, and their miseducation, Mill likened the 'labouring masses' to an 'uncultivated herd'. One consequence of their ignorance was that both men and women of the working-class family accepted the ancient institution of gender inequality 'which entirely subordinates the weaker sex to the stronger' (*CW*, 5, p. 713; 1, p. 239; and 21, p. 264). Thus although women of the educated classes might differ in this respect, the working-class women were 'consenting parties to ... the rule of men over women' because they were 'brought up from the very earliest years in the belief that their ideal of character ... [was] submission, and yielding to the control of others' (*CW*, 21, pp. 270, 271).

Mill was convinced, however, that discrimination against women was 'discordant with the future, and must necessarily disappear'. The removal of the institution of sexism was only one part of his plans for the improvement of the condition of the working class, however. And hinting at the direction that such an effort should take, he observed that he knew 'of no branch of the general culture of the mental facilities which is not a fit subject for a State provision' (*CW*, 21, p. 272; and 6, p. 227).

Reforms for the abolition of poverty

Mill's vision of the future good society, to be achieved by means of reforms, was one in which a solution had been found to the problem of how 'to unite the greatest individual liberty of action, with a common ownership in the raw materials of the globe, and an equal participation of all in the benefits of combined labour'. He 'saw clearly', however, that 'to render any such transformation either possible or desirable, an equivalent change of character must take place both in the uncultivated herd who now compose the labouring masses, and in the immense majority of their employers' (*CW*, 1, p. 239). Such a sea change of human character could be effected only by means of a system 'of national education' to be designed especially for working-class children. Given the poverty of the parents of most of those children who would benefit from educational reforms, the state would have to create, maintain and finance, not only the new schools for '*all*' children, but also 'schools for [the education of] teachers'. Such an undertaking Mill viewed as the 'highest and most important of all the objects which a government can place before itself' (*CW*, 21, p. 63).

Given the fact that Mill was convinced that the institution of the state was *the* guardian of private property and hence the wilful cause of the malignant neglect of education for and of the poor, it might be asked how he could be so optimistic as to assume that the very same state would take steps that, in the opinion of the powers that be, would undermine the institution of private property. The answer is that Mill was too careful a student of institutions to assume that the state, as *presently* constituted, would formulate and implement the necessary reforms of education. He did believe, however, that the government could be prompted at some future date to take the necessary action *if* a sufficiently powerful public demand for education should arise. '"It is to the public mind, therefore, that those who desire any change must address themselves"' (*CW*, 21, p. 64). This is exactly what Mill decided to do.

In writing on educational issues, Mill emphasized the impact of education upon the growth of population, upon the institution of property, and upon the place and role of women in society, in particular that of working-class women.

Population

In spite of the fact that '[r]eligion, morality, and statesmanship have vied with one another in incitement to marriage, and to the multiplication of the species', Mill was convinced that this cultural barrier could be scaled, but not until 'the producing [of] large families is regarded with the same feelings as drunkenness' (*CW*, 2, p. 368, 368n). Such a sentiment on the part of adults could be generated only by their education in childhood. Although he refrained from discussing in detail 'either the principles or the machinery' of the requisite education, Mill volunteered the opinion that its purpose should be to foster the idea 'among the labouring class, that the competition of too great numbers was the special cause of their poverty; so that every labourer looked ... upon every other who had more than the number of children which the circumstances of society allowed each, as doing him wrong'. Mill was therefore confident that if 'the opinion were once generally established among the labouring class that their welfare required a due regulation of the numbers of families, the respectable and well-conducted of the body would conform to the prescriptions'. The propensity to practise such regulation would be strengthened 'if women were admitted ... to the same rights of citizenship with men'. Women would be so admitted if both sexes were educated properly. They would, therefore, 'cease to be confined by custom to one physical function as their means of living and their source of influence, and they would have for the first time an equal voice with men in what concerns that function' (*CW*, 2, pp. 375, 371, 372–3).

But education for population control could not alone solve the problem of poverty. It would have to be coordinated with other types of education designed to provide the members of the working class with those abilities, skills, know-how and patterns of behaviour that they would have to command if they were to bring about that alteration of the institution of property that Mill found to be necessary if the disease of poverty were to be driven out of the body economic.

The institution of property
Mill was confident that the plight of the working class might be alleviated before long in consequence of a potential convergence of two evolving phenomena in the economy. One was a fact and the other was a potentiality. The fact was that technological advances had made labour 'more productive on the system of large industrial enterprises' than in small-scale businesses. The potential phenomenon was in the form of those newly honed faculties that the working classes would possess if Mill's recommendations for educational reforms were implemented. When the convergence materializes, Mill could not think that the workers would 'be permanently contented with the condition of labouring for wages as their ultimate state' (*CW*, 3, pp. 768, 766).

Once the workers' formal education was supplemented by informal education on the job in large-scale factories where they learned to cooperate, they would be ready to shed their status as wage earners. Mill was therefore convinced that once formal and informal education converges with modern technology, 'there can be little doubt that the *status* of hired labourers will gradually tend to confine itself to the description of workpeople whose low moral qualities render them unfit for anything independent'. The well educated workers, on the other hand, will enter into 'partnership[s], in one of two forms; in some cases, association of the labourers with the capitalists; in others … associations of labourers among themselves'. Mill was confident, however, that 'if mankind continue to improve', the form of association that must 'be expected in the end to predominate' will be the 'association of the labourers themselves on terms of equality, collectively owning the capital with which they carry on their operations, and working under managers elected and removable by themselves' (*CW*, 3, pp. 769, 775).

In Mill's opinion, large-scale producers' cooperatives are more efficient than large-scale corporations. In the first place, cooperatives are managed more efficiently than corporations. In the latter, 'the directors are very often not chosen with the necessary degree of discrimination, and [they] are not sufficiently superintended because the shareholders have other occupations, and the sum they have invested is probably but a small part of what they have'. In the cooperatives, on the other hand, the 'capital would be employed in carrying on a business with which all the persons concerned are alike familiar', a business 'which they know better than anything else, and which they are daily occupied about'. Consequently, they would 'keep a much better control over the managers, and ... be much better judges of who would be the best managers' (*CW*, 5, pp. 425–6). Second, the cooperative form of organization 'tends, still more efficaciously, to increase the productiveness of labour' because of the 'vast stimulus [it] give[s] to productive energies, by placing the labourers, as a mass, in a relation to their work which would make it their principle and their interest – at present it is neither – to do the utmost, instead of the least possible, in exchange for their remuneration'. Aggregate production would be boosted still further if cooperative wholesale and retail societies were established to distribute the outputs of producers' cooperatives because the presently 'inordinate numbers' of 'mere distributors, who are not producers but auxiliaries of production' would be 'reduced to more modest dimensions'. Hence 'a vast number of hands will be set free for production' (*CW*, 3, pp. 791–2).

Impressive as these gains would be, they would be 'nothing compared with the moral revolution' that would occur in consequence of the movement from traditional capitalism to a cooperative system. It would 'heal the standing feud between capital and labour' and give the workers 'a new sense of security and independence' and transform 'each human being's daily occupation into a school of the social sympathies and the practical intelligence' (*CW*, 3, p. 792).

Mill also recommended that the state facilitate the transformation of the institution of property by passing legislation permitting the formation of cooperative 'associations by the working classes to carry on, as their own capitalists, their own employment'. But what of financing? Mill did not have much to say in this regard. It seems that he was of the opinion that the workers themselves would be capable of providing some savings for investment in their own enterprises. 'I think', he said, that 'there is much more advantage to be gained to the working classes by this than by any other mode of investing their savings'. Mill also seems to have been of the opinion that some of the members of the professional classes might lend some of their savings to cooperatives. Thus he observed that the 'security for good management' in these institutions might prove attractive to those outside the working classes 'whose savings are small'. Once a cooperative is a going concern, its expansion could be financed by its 'members who, instead of consuming their share of the proceeds, might choose to save it, and add it to the capital of the association' (*CW*, 5, pp. 425, 410, 411).

This would be the beginning of the end of the capitalist institution of property:

> As [cooperative] associations multiplied, they would tend more and more to absorb all work-people, except those who have too little understanding, or too little virtue, to be capable of learning to act on any other system than that of narrow selfishness. As this change proceeded, owners of capital would gradually find it to their advantage, instead of maintaining the struggle of the old system with work-people of only the worst description, to lend their capital to the associations; to do this at a diminishing rate of interest, and at last, perhaps, even to exchange their capital for terminable annuities [issued by the cooperative associations]. (*CW*, 3, p. 793)

Once the institution of property has been transformed from a capitalist to a cooperative mode, Mill was confident that we 'would realize, at least in the industrial department, the best aspirations of the democratic spirit, by putting an end to the division of society into the industrious and the idle, and effacing all social distinctions but those fairly earned by personal services and exertions' (*CW*, 3, p. 793).

The position of women

If Mill's proposal for educational reforms were implemented, they would produce a change not only in men's attitudes toward women but also in women's attitude toward themselves and their position in society. Hence Mill was of the opinion that the 'first and indispensable step ... towards the enfranchisement [and liberation] of woman, is that she be so educated, as not to be dependent either on her father or her husband for subsistence' (*CW*, 21, p. 42). Echoing his wife, Harriet Taylor Mill (Taylor in *CW*, 21, p. 400), Mill declared that the resultant 'opening of industrial occupations freely to both sexes' would have the effect, not only of increasing aggregate production, but also of removing a hitherto 'forced dissimilarity of [the] social functions' of the two sexes. Moreover, the 'industrial and social independence of women' would greatly reduce the 'evil of overpopulation. It is by devoting one-half of the human species to that function, by making it fill the entire life of one sex, and interweave itself with almost all of the objects of the other, that the animal instinct in question is nursed into the disproportionate preponderance which it has hitherto exercised in human life'. The gainful employment of women would reduce that preponderance. '[P]opulation, therefore, will bear a gradually diminishing ratio to capital and employment' (*CW*, 3, pp. 765, 766).

Mill's predictions

Mill was confident that, if implemented, his proposals for reform would prevent the materialization of David Ricardo's feared 'stagnant sea' of a dismal 'stationary state'. A stationary state would come about, but it would be a virtuous one. Instead of making 'the industrial arts' serve 'no purpose but the increase of wealth, industrial improvements would produce their legitimate effect, that of abridging labour'. Hence the virtuous stationary state of the future would 'exhibit these leading features' (*CW*, 3, pp. 752, 756, 755):

> a well-paid and affluent body of labourers; no enormous fortunes, ... but a much larger body of persons than at present, not only exempt from the coarser toils, but with sufficient leisure, both physical and mental, from mechanical details, to cultivate freely the graces of life. ... This condition of society, so greatly preferable to the present, is not only perfectly compatible with the stationary state, but, it would seem, more naturally allied with that state than with any other. (*CW*, 3, p. 755)

Mill concluded, therefore, that '[o]nly when, in addition to just institutions, the increase of mankind shall be under the deliberate guidance of judicious foresight, can the conquest made from the powers of nature by the intellectual energy of scientific discoverers, become the common property of the species, and the means of improving and elevating the universal lot' (*CW*, 3, p. 757).

Conclusion

Although he may not be an 'institutionalist' in the sense in which the practitioners of the 'old institutionalism' in the tradition of Thorstein B. Veblen and John R. Commons are institutionalists, nor in the sense in which Oliver E. Williamson, Douglass C. North and their followers in the 'new institutionalism' are institutionalists,[6] Mill may be called an institutionalist for two closely related reasons. In the first place, he did undertake an inquiry into the nature, character and behaviour of those institutions that he found to be of crucial importance in the economic order. Second, he employed his institutionalist analysis, and the conclusions that he drew therefrom, as supporting pillars for his classical economics. In so doing, he transformed Ricardo's classical 'agricultural' economics into a classical 'labour' economics. And Mill did so in order to explain how it might be possible for the working classes, men and women, to achieve self-realization through an improvement of their human capital that would make it possible for them to change their economic condition for the better and to enjoy a measure of social justice that had been denied to their forebears.

It hardly needs to be observed that Mill was overly optimistic, even utopian, in his belief in the efficacy of education as a means to the improvement of the human character and hence to the end of completely humanizing the institutions of society. In this respect, he out-institutionalised both the 'old' and the 'new' institutionalists of the twentieth century.

Notes

1. The author wishes to thank Chris Guest, Oskar Kurer, Ingrid H. Rima and Warren J. Samuels for their helpful critical comments on an earlier draft. The usual caveats apply.
2. References to Mill's works are to the *Collected Works of John Stuart Mill*, abbreviated as *CW*, followed by volume number and page number(s).
3. See C.E. Ayres (1952), pp. 42–50, Paul D. Bush (1983), and William T. Waller, Jr (1982).
4. As Ayres put it, when people move into a 'frontier region' from an 'older center of civilization', the 'mores and folkways' that they bring with them 'invariably suffer some reduction in importance under the conditions of frontier life' (Ayres, 1944, p. 133).
5. Thus it seems that Mill anticipated the modern theories of imperfect competition as well as the institutionalist theory of the separation of ownership and control that was formulated by Adolf A. Berle, Jr and Gardiner C. Means in the early 1930s (Berle and Means, 1932).
6. For comparisons of the old and the new institutionalism, see Coats (1990), Hodgson (1989), Mayhew (1989), Rutherford (1989), and Samuels (1990).

References

Ayres, C.E. (1944), *The Theory of Economic Progress*, Chapel Hill: The University of North Carolina Press.

Ayres, C.E. (1952), *The Industrial Economy*, Boston: Houghton Mifflin.

Berle, Adolf A., Jr and Gardiner C. Means (1932), *The Modern Corporation and Private Property*, New York: Macmillan.

Bush, Paul D. (1983), 'An Exploration of the Structural Characteristics a Veblen–Ayres–Foster Defined Institutional Domain', *Journal of Economic Issues*, **17**, March, pp. 35–66.

Carlisle, Janice (1991), *John Stuart Mill and the Writing of Character*, Athens: The University of Georgia Press.

Coats, A.W. (1990), 'Confrontation in Toronto: reactions to the "old" versus the "new" institutionalism session', *Review of Political Economy*, **2**, March, pp. 87–93.

Hodgson, Geoffrey M. (1989), 'Institutional economic theory: the old versus the new', *Review of Political Economy*, **1**, November, pp. 249–69.

Mayhew, Anne (1989), 'Contrasting origins of the two institutionalisms: the social science context', *Review of Political Economy*, **1**, November, pp. 319–33.

Mill, James (1967), *Analysis of the Phenomenon of the Human Mind*, 2 vols, 2nd ed. Edited with additional notes by John Stuart Mill, New York: Augustus M. Kelley.

Mill, John Stuart (1963–91), *Collected Works of John Stuart Mill*, Toronto: University of Toronto Press. The cited volumes are arranged by volume number.

   1. (1981), *Autobiography and Literary Essays*, ed. John M. Robson and Jack Stillinger.
   2. (1965), *Principles of Political Economy*, Books I–II, ed. J.M. Robson.
   3. (1965), *Principles of Political Economy*, Books III–IV and Appendices, ed. J.M. Robson.
   4. (1967), *Essays on Economics and Society 1824–1845*, ed. J.M. Robson.
   5. (1967), *Essays on Economics and Society 1850–1879*, ed. J.M. Robson.
   6. (1982), *Essays on England, Ireland and the Empire*, ed. J.M. Robson.
   9. (1979), *An Examination of Sir William Hamilton's Philosophy and the Principal Questions Discussed in his Writings*, ed. J.M. Robson.
  10. (1969), *Essays on Ethics, Religion and Society*, ed. J.M. Robson.
  18. (1977), *Essays on Politics and Society*, ed. J.M. Robson.
  21. (1984), *Essays on Equality, Law, and Education*, ed. J.M. Robson.
  26. (1988), *Journal and Debating Speeches*, ed. J.M. Robson.
  28. (1988), *Public and Parliamentary Speeches November 1850–November 1868*, ed. J.M. Robson and B.L. Kinzer.
  31. (1989), *Miscellaneous Writings*, ed. J.M. Robson.

Rutherford, Malcolm (1989), 'What is wrong with the new institutional economics (and what is still wrong with the old)?', *Review of Political Economy*, **1**, November, pp. 299–318.

Samuels, Warren J. (1990), 'The old versus the new institutionalism', *Review of Political Economy*, **2**, March, pp. 83–6.

Waller, William T. (1982), 'The Evolution of the Veblenian Dichotomy: Veblen, Hamilton, Ayres, and Foster', *Journal of Economic Issues*, **16**, September, pp. 757–71.
Wilson, Fred (1990), *Psychological Analysis and the Philosophy of John Stuart Mill*, Toronto: University of Toronto Press.

7 The role of perfect foresight in Krishna Bharadwaj's critique of demand and supply equilibrium-based theory

Harvey Gram

Introduction – two theories of value and distribution

Krishna Bharadwaj argued throughout her work[1] that a clear distinction can be drawn between two different theories of value and distribution: a surplus-based analysis seen, in its modern form, as underlying the work of Smith, Ricardo and Marx, in contradistinction to the now dominant demand and supply equilibrium-based theory (hereafter, DSE-based theory), developed during the first half of the nineteenth century and later spearheaded in the writings of Jevons, Menger and Walras.[2] The shift away from a surplus-based analysis towards a DSE-based theory is attributed, in part, to the inability of Ricardo successfully to defend his theory of the rate of profit against criticisms, and, later, to the influence of Ricardo's followers who, for various reasons (some, no doubt, politically motivated), began to support the idea that profit was a payment corresponding to the real cost of 'abstinence'. This idea reached its apotheosis in the writings of Alfred Marshall, himself inspired by von Thünen and Cournot, rather than by Ricardo, and who regarded his own early work as an effort to treat formally, in so far as that was possible, John Stuart Mill's *Principles of Political Economy*, 'wherein both the rate of wages and profits (the latter themselves viewed as a recompense for abstinence) were considered *independent determinants* of value' (Bharadwaj, 1989, p. 65). Indeed, Marshall is portrayed by Bharadwaj as having done more by means of his generous interpretations to subvert Ricardo's doctrines than Jevons was able to do by ignoring them, giving all the emphasis in his praise of older ideas to the classical theory of rent: 'a theory of distinctly mathematical character, *which seems to give a clue to the correct mode of treating the whole science* (Jevons, 1911, p. vi, cited, with emphasis added, by Bharadwaj, 1989, p. 156, n.9).

The distinction between surplus-based and DSE-based theories turns on the identification of a basic structure common to each theory. Inspired by Piero Sraffa's *Production of Commodities by Means of Commodities*, an 'investigation … concerned exclusively with such properties of an economic system as do not depend on changes in the scale of production or in the proportions of "factors"' (Sraffa, 1960, p. v; cited by Bharadwaj, 1989, p. 222),

93

Bharadwaj takes the position that the parameters of a surplus-based theory should include: the level and composition of output; the observed and therefore 'dominant' methods of production; and the 'historically' determined real wage. This extraordinary list of *givens*, extraordinary, that is, from the point of view of conventional resource allocation theory, provides the basis for defining a set of exchange values consistent with the circular reproduction and possible expansion of an economic system – a system in which commodities are produced by means of commodities and in which the surplus output, over and above what is necessary for the reproduction of the economy's material base (including its labour force), is allocated to the owners of the capital stock according to particular, socially defined 'rules of circulation'. In the simplest case, these rules reflect competitive behaviour and find expression in the uniformity of prices for each separate commodity together with a uniform rate of profit and a uniform wage for each type of labour skill. Nothing precludes introduction into this framework of: elements of monopoly pricing; systematic variations in profit rates due to 'differences as in "security, cleanliness", etc. of different employments (as in Adam Smith)' (Bharadwaj, 1989, p. 92); or systematic differences in wage rates occasioned by differences in the training costs associated with various employments. The set of exchange values consistent with reproduction of the technical and social relations of production are seen by Bharadwaj as the 'natural prices' of classical theory 'rooted in historical experience and not entirely "abstract"' (Bharadwaj, 1989, p. 25) since the 'quantities' on the basis of which they are derived, namely, 'effectual demand', dominant methods of production, and historically given wages, are 'derived as "average characteristics" of the economy, on the basis of observations' (Bharadwaj, 1989, p. 25).[3]

Bharadwaj emphasized that the 'natural prices' of classical theory are not to be confused with the prices corresponding to Marshall's *long-period equilibrium* wherein profit is an element of cost rather than a residual payment to the owners of the capital stock. Neither are the market prices of classical theory, 'viewed as deviations from natural prices caused by accidental factors affecting conditions of supply and demand' (Bharadwaj, 1989, p. 192) to be seen as corresponding to a *short-period equilibrium* in which substitution effects come into play as the mechanism which equates supply and demand. Market prices in classical theory are not amenable to systematic analysis because of the diverse, transient factors which affect them. Nevertheless, a divergence between market prices and natural prices manifests itself in terms of 'temporary differences in profits ... [which] would set into motion "apportionment of capital" whereby the tendency towards profit rate equalization asserts itself' (Bharadwaj, 1989, p. 99). Bharadwaj noted Ricardo's reservation that 'It is perhaps very difficult to trace the steps by which this change is effected'. She did not, however, refer to more recent efforts, such as those of

Goodwin (1970) and Goodwin and Punzo (1987), to analyse the 'cross field dynamics' or 'dual linear dynamics' of simultaneous price and quantity adjustment within a classical framework of analysis. Commenting on Adam Smith's discussion of 'market price' as 'regulated by "the proportion between the quantity which is actually brought to market, and the demand of those who are willing to pay the natural price of the commodity"', Bharadwaj noted that in *The Wealth of Nations* there is no 'universal theory about the operation of the substitution principle, whereby relative commodity proportions vary in response to changes in relative prices' (Bharadwaj, 1989, p. 27).

In contrast to her somewhat cursory remarks concerning the problem of 'gravitation' of market prices toward 'natural prices', Bharadwaj emphasizes the openness – some would say the indeterminateness – of a surplus-based theory which takes as given the level and composition of output, the dominant method of production and the real wage. Her purpose is to suggest that, rather than being 'unduly restrictive', the separation implied by a 'prior' determination of the above-mentioned quantities has an advantage over the simultaneous determination of prices and quantities characteristic of DSE-based theory. It opens up

the possibility of introducing a wider range of determinants and the real dynamics of the process of change; precisely because, thereby, the more complex, historically specific, institutional and social forces that govern changes (particularly in distribution, technology of production, and investment) can be introduced. While prices may, in turn, influence quantities, it is recognized that there are even more significant factors directly influencing quantities that may be considered to operate fairly independently of changes in relative prices. ... Adam Smith's treatment of the relation between the division of labour and the extent of the market; [and] Marx's discussion of qualitative and quantitative changes in capital/labour relations, influencing, and being influenced by, technical change. Keynes's analysis of the multiplier could be said to follow the same approach. (Bharadwaj, 1989, p. 244)

A critique of demand and supply equilibrium-based theory
The DSE-based theories which Bharadwaj saw as gradually undermining and finally displacing altogether the surplus-based approach have a familiar structure. The parametric givens of this theory are: 'initial resource endowments and their distribution among individuals, the technological possibilities and the system of preferences' (Bharadwaj, 1989, p. 7). This theory

visualizes the economy as an aggregate of atomistic individuals (producers and consumers) making their decisions autonomously, with no interference from the influence of 'externalities'. Relative prices and quantities are determined simultaneously in equilibrium as an outcome of the interplay of 'forces of demand and supply', generated by the optimizing behaviour of individuals subject to their resource constraints. A certain symmetry characterizes the behaviour of producers and consumers. ... It is through the operation of the 'fundamental' and 'universal' principle of substitution that individuals adjust their chosen quantities in response to variations in the parametrically given prices. The relative prices formed on the market vary in response to excess demands or supplies in particular markets in such a way as to clear all markets in equilibrium. (Bharadwaj, 1989, p. 7)

Much of Bharadwaj's critique of DSE-based theories is concerned with the ways in which it has been used to interpret the writings of Smith, Ricardo and Marx, leading to misunderstandings and misinterpretations of the central concepts of a surplus-based theory. Thus, 'the classical distinction (which was a qualitative one) between "market" and "natural variables" was reformulated as a distinction between "short-period" and "long-period" equilibria' (Bharadwaj, 1989, p. 6). Bharadwaj is not objecting to the fact that gravitation towards a natural position will take time or that the terms 'short-period' and 'long-period' might be used in a discussion of how an economy 'accommodate[s] fresh observations of economic phenomena' (Bharadwaj, 1989, p. 6). She is objecting, rather, to the idea that the *only* difference between a short-period and a long-period equilibrium, that is to say, the only difference that a DSE-based theory credits to the classical distinction between 'market' and 'natural' values is the *extent* or *degree* to which the principle of substitution in response to price changes has come into play. Indeed, a recurring theme in Bharadwaj's essays concerns the enervating effect of this one idea, which, of course, many economists would regard as the whole basis for their claim to be engaging in a scientific, and peculiarly economic approach to the various social problems with which they are concerned.

Although she did not play her trump card as often as one might have expected, Bharadwaj did refer on several occasions to 'the recent debates in capital theory which highlighted certain logical difficulties faced by the theory, especially in the determination of the rate of profit. The difficulty arose primarily in the form of a failure to ensure a well-behaved demand function for capital, mainly because a theoretically adequate measure of capital, independent of distribution, could not be constructed' (Bharadwaj, 1989, p. 188).

The difficulty ... arises because the supply-and-demand theories seek to explain distribution within their price-determination schema and the assumption of initially given resources leads to certain logical inconsistencies within that framework: when capital is considered as a given value-sum, independent of distribution, the problem appears to be that of generating a 'normally' shaped demand function for capital; when, on the other hand, it is considered as a list of quantities of heterogeneous assets, the problem is to ensure uniformity of the rate of profit in the long-run equilibrium. (Bharadwaj, 1989, p. 199)

Why has this result of the capital theory controversy not been regarded by mainstream theorists as fatal to their DSE-based framework of analysis? In looking for the answer, it is essential to have in mind a class of models for that theory which is capable of standing up to criticism, that is, a class of models which would, in fact, be defended against the charge that its explanation of distribution 'leads to certain logical inconsistencies'. Forward-looking models of intertemporal optimization in which equilibrium over time is the organizing principle define such a class.[4]

The role of perfect foresight

Bharadwaj recognized the seminal role of Irving Fisher in extending the concept of a balance of forces of supply and demand to encompass the passage of time. Although Fisher denied the importance of the classical notion of cost of production, he did not give up the method of long-period analysis.[5] In *The Nature of Capital and Income*, he states that 'When prices find their normal level at which costs plus interest are covered, it is not because the past costs of production have determined prices in advance, but because the sellers have been good speculators as to what prices would be' (Fisher, 1906, p. 188; cited by Bharadwaj, 1989, p. 233). Prices are expected to find their normal cost-determined level, and yet the process which brings this about is based on correct foresight about the future. In Fisher's words, 'the causal relation is ... not from present to future but future to present' (Fisher, 1906, p. 328; cited by Bharadwaj, 1989, p. 249, n.21).

The Fisherian notion that equilibrium entails accurate speculative behaviour finds formal expression in forward-looking intertemporal DSE-based models. Avinash Dixit (1990) notes that the theoretical analysis of production and capital accumulation within general equilibrium theory 'achieved its lift-off when Cass (1965), Shell (1967) and others used a mixture of fuels: the aggregative growth model and Pontryagin's maximum principle' (Dixit, 1990, p. 5) to generate equilibrium paths which are entirely forward-looking and, in that sense, ahistorical. A central feature of such models – a feature which was once seen as exposing the futility of applying the concept of supply and demand equilibrium to the problem of capital accumulation within a multi-period setting – concerns the *saddle-point property* of the long-period position. As Edwin Burmeister remarks,

> [W]e shall find that the rest points for the dynamic equations of multisector models generally are saddle-points in the space of capital good prices ... and per capita capital stocks. When this saddlepoint property exists, for any given initial vector of [capital stocks], the model converges ... only for a *particular* choice of initial price vector. (Burmeister, 1980, p. 214)

No longer a 'centre of gravity', relative to which prices and quantities fluctuate, long-period equilibrium in intertemporal DSE-based theory is a position which can only be reached along a saddle-path by assuming a particular *initial* set of market-clearing prices. The *theory* picks out an initial price vector such that convergence to some steady-state equilibrium (or limit cycle) is guaranteed (Burmeister, 1980, p. 236).

The theoretical quandary made evident by the saddle-point property of a long-period intertemporal equilibrium of demand and supply, and the associated saddle-path leading to that point, is the consequence of a well known problem associated with a 'short-period general equilibrium of demand and supply compatible with given quantities of ... several capital goods' (Garegnani, 1976, p. 138). In such an equilibrium, *net returns* to the ownership of various capital goods, defined as market or 'shadow' rental rates for the 'services' of capital goods divided by their respective supply prices (minus their respective rates of depreciation), will generally differ. 'The competitive tendency to a uniform rate of profits will be powerful and quick in bringing about changes in the composition of the capital stock and, hence ... appreciable changes in the prices of productive services and commodities' (Garegnani, 1976, p. 139). The postulate required for a coherent theory of demand and supply equilibrium is that *initial prices* are such that outputs of capital goods (satisfying the equilibrium requirement that the value of total production should be a maximum) result in *changes* in the production possibilities set which, in turn, bring about 'appropriate' changes in the prices of those very same capital goods in the next time period. 'Appropriate' means that, from one period to the next, the capital gains or losses on the holding of any particular capital good, when *added* to its net return (defined above), will result in an equalization of yields on all such assets. Given a single consumption good and an appropriately restricted intertemporal consumption function, this common yield is simultaneously equal to the interest rate implicit in the marginal rate of intertemporal substitution.

The saddle-path property of the trajectory leading to a long-period demand and supply equilibrium brings out clearly the fact that, in this theory, there can be no out-of-equilibrium *tendency*, associated with the competitive behaviour of capitalists, toward equalization of the rate of profit in different lines of activity. This tendency, an essential characteristic of the long-period method of the classical economists, has been sacrificed to the requirements of a DSE-based theory. Thus a changing, but always uniform rate of return (inclusive of correctly anticipated capital gains and losses) reflects a continuing balance between the forces of 'productivity', in the form of an ever-changing, but always 'well-behaved' production possibilities set, and 'thrift', represented by a given intertemporal utility function. All this, and a present discounted value of the capital stock which remains *constant* from beginning to end (Dorfman, Samuelson and Solow, 1958, pp. 321–2), is implicit in the theoretically determined initial price vector.[6] Any other initial prices eventually result in a non-uniform yield on capital

assets: in particular, an infinite rate of return on assets with zero prices.[7]
Burmeister notes:

> Such 'errant' nonconvergent paths generating this inconsistency [non-uniform
> rates of return, assuming 'competitive', price-taking behaviour by cost-minimiz-
> ing firms, and non-negative capital good prices] can be ruled out [when the long-
> run saddle-point is unique] if *all* contracts are made at time [zero]. If ... all
> intertemporal decisions are concluded at time zero ... nonconvergent paths along
> which equilibrium in the markets for capital assets is violated in finite time are not
> admissible. In such a fictitious world convergence to the unique saddlepoint
> equilibrium is assured. Such 'solutions' must be rejected if our objective is to
> better understand the operation of real-world economies, for obviously economic
> transactions are continuously occurring. (Burmeister, 1980, p. 228)

Paul Samuelson, in discussing a 'descriptive' (as opposed to an 'optimal')
growth model with a long-period saddle-point equilibrium solution
(Samuelson, 1967) goes further in his critical remarks, appearing to reject the
equilibrium theory of demand and supply altogether when faced with its
logical implications. Under the heading, 'Reaiming Behavior of Speculators',
he abandons the formal strictures of the theory while attempting to salvage
some insight with a carefully chosen metaphor.

> The image in my mind is that of a bicycle. The rider of the bicycle is the bulk of
> the market, a somewhat mystical concept to be sure – like its analogue, the well-
> informed speculator who gets his way in the end because his way is the correctly
> discerned way of the future; and those who think differently are bankrupted by
> their bets against (him and) the future. (It is easier to identify the well-informed
> speculator *ex post* than *ex ante* and the image can easily dissolve into an empty
> tautology.) ... [W]hen the system is led too far from the balanced-growth configu-
> ration, some entrepreneurs begin to foresee the shoals ahead ... and they act to
> push the system back toward the turnpike. Even if there is something valid in this
> heuristic reasoning, one must admit that the system need not – and, generally, will
> not – move from its present position to the golden age in the most efficient way: it
> will hare after false goals, get detoured, and begin to be corrected only after it has
> erred. (Samuelson, 1967, p. 229)

Until recently, 'saddle-point instability'[8] was taken to mean that the underlying model was appropriate only to a planning environment in which some
external institution would be in charge of what Samuelson has called the
'aiming problem'. Burmeister summarizes this conventional view: 'This feature [saddle-point instability] is not worrisome in a planning context where
initial prices are assigned to assure such convergence along an optimal path
or where convergence is not in itself an economic issue' (Burmeister, 1980,
p. 264). Otherwise, DSE-based models would stand precariously on the un-
explained dominance of speculators with correct information about future
events. Nowadays, such doubts are rarely expressed. Dixit writes:

> When the saddle-point instability of equilibrium paths in the phase space was first discovered, it was thought to be potentially fatal to the whole theory. ... Many papers were written that sought to understand this difficulty, or to resolve it. Nowadays the saddle-point property is generally taken to be a positive help in *pinning down the initial prices*. As a practical researcher who likes to get results, I adopt the new view, but cannot occasionally help remembering the serious concerns behind the old one. (Dixit, 1990, p. 6, emphasis added)

Here is a remarkably candid statement of the misgivings which accompany the need, as Bharadwaj notes, to choose 'assumptions which were *not derived on the basis of historical observation, but were merely postulates required for the theory*' (Bharadwaj, 1989, p. 233).[9]

Neoclassical theory in a straightjacket
A coherent model of supply and demand equilibrium requires expectations to be continuously realized, subject at most to serially uncorrelated random errors. Disequilibrium is ruled out even in the short run: to allow *any* time for adjustments to unforeseen events is to allow *too much* time. Thus, in response to parameter shifts, a DSE-based model incorporating perfect foresight or its stochastic counterpart (rational expectations) requires instantaneous and precisely determined shifts in expected prices, actual prices and rates of change of quantities.[10] Replacing capital good prices with their expectations (regarded, subjectively, as certain) appears to have yielded little progress in solving the saddle-point instability problem despite the claim that 'a satisfactory resolution that is realistic necessitates the explicit introduction of stochastic features into the model' (Burmeister, 1980, p. 214).

Intertemporal DSE-based theory clearly denies a long-standing interpretation of market prices, common to both classical and neoclassical theory (in its original form), namely, as signals communicating information about opportunities for profitable production and exchange. These opportunities – which provide the foundation for the analytical significance of the long-period method of the classical economists – simply never arise. Professor Leijonhufvud notes the 'general proposition that the rational expectations literature is making exceedingly familiar; namely that fully informed agents have no need for a price mechanism to inform them about what is happening. Prices merely reflect what they already know' (Leijonhufvud, 1983, p. 80). In spite of this extraordinarily negative conclusion, there appears to be a consensus that a general equilibrium of supply and demand is the touchstone for acceptable theory in both microeconomics and macroeconomics.[11] Nicholas Kaldor saw in this commitment something almost mystical: 'It is the deep underlying *belief*, common to all economists of the so-called "neo-classical" school, that general equilibrium theory is the one and only starting point for any logically consistent explanation of the behaviour of de-centralized economic systems' (Kaldor, 1972, p. 1238).

The insuperable difficulties which accompany every effort to extend into the unobservable future the terrain over which the equilibrium theory of demand and supply holds sway are generally set aside as problems which will somehow ultimately yield to a more sophisticated analysis. Who takes seriously the suggestion of Professor Hahn that while not 'denying the great merit of [general equilibrium theory] in settling a particular intellectual debate one may well wish to argue that the time has come to start from scratch' (Hahn, 1984, p. 140)? The few who do either ignore or misinterpret, as a special uninteresting case of their own theory, the long-period method of the classical economists. On this view, post-Sraffian theory is of slight interest at best, and at worst a source of mischievous, ideologically motivated, error. Hahn remarks that Sraffa's *Production of Commodities by Means of Commodities* 'was both careful and completely honest. He was wrong to link the general impossibility of perfect capital aggregation with marginal productivity theory but he had aggregate 'parables' in mind. In all other respects the book ... contained little that was new or objectionable to practioners of linear models' (Hahn, 1984, p. 17). The 'little that was new' concerned the phenomenon of reswitching of techniques from which it followed that 'we cannot say that one technique is more capital intensive than another *and* that capital intensity is inversely related to [the rate of profit]' (Hahn, 1984, p. 383). In a similar vein, Burmeister proves, within the framework of an intertemporal general equilibrium model, that reswitching only *complicates* the study of time-paths of adjustment (Burmeister, 1980, pp. 203–9); while Dixit simply asserts, in his effort to 'dismiss [the capital theoretic aspect] quickly and move on to more important things ..., [that] ideological issues ... somehow got entangled in the capital theory controversy in the late 1960s and early 1970s' (Dixit, 1990, p. 4).

The widely recognized difficulties encountered in attempts to 'dynamize' DSE-based models show how that theory has painted itself into a box from which there is no escape. Bharadwaj does not mention the problem of saddle-point instability, referring only once, in a footnote, to the problem of 'getting into equilibrium': 'Another critique of "fundamental Keynesians" ... concerns "the equilibrium method", which argues that the logical conditions defining the notion of equilibrium connote a state of affairs either unapproachable or unattainable, unless the economy is already in it. ... Joan Robinson returned to this theme repeatedly, contrasting history with equilibrium' (Bharadwaj, 1989, p. 247, n.1; see also p. 292, section 5.12). The view taken here is that, in light of developments which have taken place during the last three decades within DSE-based theory, the assumption of perfect foresight or its stochastic counterpart, rational expectations, is a more relevant object of criticism than the assumptions concerning particular and limited forms of substitution in response to price changes which Bharadwaj takes to be the essential weakness underlying DSE-based theory.[12]

Classical theory – some open questions

Taking these limitations as understood, but somehow overlooked by 'a practical researcher who likes to get results' (Dixit, 1990, p. 6), it remains true that, from the point of view of DSE-based theory, the long-period method of the classical economists, as interpreted by Bharadwaj, remains hopelessly underdetermined and therefore incapable of generating 'results'.

A theory of the 'givens' of classical theory must begin with a theory of demand if it is to explain 'the level and composition of social output' (Bharadwaj, 1989, p. 25). DSE-based theory simply postulates a list of '*n* commodities', remaining silent on the question of where this 'menu' comes from. A modern classical theory asks, 'Who writes the menu?'. The time is long overdue to take seriously Marshall's concern that 'the prominent place which consumption has received in the programme of the science has not been justified by any attempt to examine it carefully' and to recognize that 'this neglect [has not] been altogether accidental' (Marshall, 1890; cited by Bharadwaj, 1989, p. 229). It has rather been a consequence of the effort to place production and consumption on symmetrical foundations reflecting price-induced substitution. Experiments have shown that animals respond to 'price signals' in such a way as to confirm the substitution effect, but perhaps for that very reason, it is time to recognize Marshall's caveat that 'while wants are the rulers of life among lower animals, it is to changes in the form of effort and activities that we must turn when in search for the keystones of the history of mankind' (Marshall, 1920, p. 85; cited by Bharadwaj, 1989, pp. 230–31). The role of the state in modern industrial economies, long recognized as fundamental to the determination of the 'level and composition of social output' must also be analysed, as must the role of firms in deciding what *new* commodities to produce and what associated levels of investment in plant and equipment and expenditures on advertising to undertake. It is in this context that a Keynesian theory of effective demand can be integrated into modern classical theory without resort to contrived arguments concerning 'failures of coordination' caused by 'price signals' which are incomplete or incorrect *from the point of view of DSE-based theory*.

The link between 'the level and composition of social output' and 'the "given" methods of production' (Bharadwaj, 1989, p. 182), which is essential to the determination of long-period 'natural' prices, rests on a theory of technological change. To suppose that the 'best practice' technique is the dominant and therefore relevant one is inadequate as it presupposes the very process of invention, innovation, and diffusion which must be the subject of inquiry. It is here that 'the common sense meaning [of competition as a] struggle with others, of fight, of attempting to get ahead, or at least to hold one's place' (Morgenstern, 1972, p. 1164; cited by Bharadwaj, 1989, p. 20, n.55) must get a hearing. A difficult task, to be sure, but at least a modern classical model allows room for what Kaldor referred to as the 'creative function' of markets (cited by Bharadwaj, 1989, p. 247, n.1). DSE-based theories appear to finesse the problem of technological change by supposing that resources and technology are separable parameters. One cannot know what a 'resource' is until 'technology' and the process by which it develops are specified. It is inadequate simply to postulate 'm factor services' in which case 'resources' can only mean the quantities listed on a preconceived menu of ingredients.

Finally, both the level and composition of output and the technique in use must be consistent with the 'bundle of commodities' which counts as the real wage. The seeming generality of a utility function, with whatever properties prove necessary or convenient in formulating a DSE-based model, should not preclude a discussion of the historical link between the 'stages of development' of industrial societies and what counts as the 'necessities of life'. Changes in methods of production and in the way work is organized can bring about changes in 'subsistence', which is therefore historically relative.

In all these difficult endeavours, a role for market prices is by no means excluded. Their proper role, however, is in 'transmitting impulses to economic change' (Kaldor, 1972, p. 1240) rather than in reflecting what 'fully informed agents ... already know' (Leijonhufvud, 1983, p. 80).

Mainstream theorists readily grant that a general equilibrium theory of supply and demand has not proved 'helpful in studying processes whether of decisions or of information or of organisation' (Hahn, 1984, p. 140). Their interest in such processes and in theories of learning ought to provide some common ground with modern classical theorists who are attempting to re-introduce elements of social, institutional, and technological change into the mainstream of economic theory. The same may be said of developments in 'evolutionary economics' (Nelson and Winter, 1982) and 'institutional economics', both new and old (Hodgson, 1988). And yet, there is little hope for establishing any such common research agenda as long as the awareness of theoretical problems arises, not from a self-conscious consideration of the realities of economic life, but rather from an attempt to answer the conundrums thrown up by a theoretical scheme whose only way of treating the forward march of time is somehow to force the present to comprehend the future by encapsulating its unknown consequences within the confines of a pre-ordained equilibrium of supply and demand.

Notes

1. Krishna Bharadwaj's papers are collected in *Themes of Value and Distribution, Classical Theory Reappraised*, London: Unwin Hyman, 1989, to which references will be made in what follows.

2. Bharadwaj avoids the contrasting terms 'classical' and 'neoclassical', contending that classical and neoclassical theorists had essentially the *same* questions in mind – questions concerning the theory of value and distribution and its relationship to broader issues surrounding economic growth and development. To the extent that the neoclassics embraced a DSE-based theory of simultaneous price and quantity determination, they were gradually forced to adopt assumptions and postulates which made their analysis, in Bharadwaj's view, not only ahistorical, but also, in the end, illogical.

3. There is some ambiguity surrounding the notion of 'effectual demand'. In Adam Smith's usage, this notion presumed a set of 'natural prices' and is not therefore independent of what 'effectual demand' is, in part, meant to determine. Bharadwaj sometimes uses the phrase 'level and composition of social output' rather than 'effectual demand'.

4. Joan Robinson remarked that she could never make intertemporal equilibrium theory stand up long enough to knock it down.

5. Pierangelo Garegnani (1976) has written of this ambivalence in the early neoclassics. They retained the 'method' of the classical economists in the concept of a long-period position and yet altered the 'theory' concerning the relationship of market forces to such a position.

6. Note how a *constant* present discounted value of capital, *uniform* (although changing) rates of returns (inclusive of capital gains and losses), and *heterogeneous* capital goods are accommodated within this theory.

7. In passing, one may note that, even in the simplest static models of pure exchange, without production, zero prices have long been recognized as creating serious theoretical problems for a DSE-based theory. See Rizvi (1991) for a review of the literature and a general claim that DSE-based theory has relevance *only* for an economy of *self-sufficient* agents.

8. Saddle-point instability is often referred to as the 'Hahn problem' by writers referring to Hahn (1966). See, for example, Burmeister (1980), p. 227 and Dixit (1990), p. 6. This suggests a too narrow reading of Professor Hahn's work. His view is that an equilibrium of supply and demand 'makes no formal or explicit causal claims at all' (Hahn, 1984, p. 47). However, just as Burmeister sees the lack of a complete set of futures markets as the source of the difficulty with the theory, which, by implication, would otherwise be completely coherent, Hahn suggests that what is missing from the otherwise meaningless analysis of 'stability' of a supply and demand equilibrium is a theory of 'learning' (Hahn, 1984, Part I). In a similar vein, Franklin Fisher comments (although he does not refer to her) on what Joan Robinson called the problem of 'getting into equilibrium': 'The theory of value is not satisfactory without a description of the adjustment processes that are applicable to the economy and of the way in which individual agents adjust to disequilibrium. In this sense, stability analysis is of far more than merely technical interest. It is the first step in a reformulation of the theory of value' (Fisher, 1983, p. 16).

9. In the context of this remark, Bharadwaj is particularly attuned to Marshall's doubts concerning the applicability and generality of his own theory.

10. In certain deterministic and stochastic models, the 'saddle-point instability' problem does not arise when market prices adjust *sufficiently slowly*. However, slow adjustment, in so far as it depends on slow adaptation, is now rejected by many theorists. 'The adaptive expectations hypothesis is subject to the compelling criticism that it implies the unreasonable conclusion that economic agents do not use all the information available to them' (Burmeister, 1980, p. 309, n.13).

11. Curiously, Professor Hahn, despite his wide-ranging criticisms of general equilibrium theory, has described the Arrow–Debreu model as 'complete' (Hahn, 1984, p. 44), 'the best base camp for sallies into new territory' (Hahn, 1984, p. 10).

12. This is not to say that other aspects of DSE-based theory are not even more damaging to

its claim to being, if not a universally relevant framework of analysis, at least the best starting point for such an analysis. Its reductionist point of view is an obvious target and would have to be discussed in any answer to the suggestion, implicit in Dixit's brief commentary on the capital theory controversy, that DSE-based theory is somehow *non-*ideological. Another large issue concerns the philosophical problem surrounding the question of what it means to optimize over an uncertain future.

References

Bharadwaj, Krishna (1989), *Themes in Value and Distribution, Classical Theory Reappraised*, London: Unwin Hyman.

Burmeister, Edwin (1980), *Capital Theory and Dynamics*, Cambridge: Cambridge University Press.

Cass, David (1965), 'Optimum Growth in an Aggregative Model of Capital Accumulation', *Review of Economic Studies*, **32**, pp. 233–40.

Dixit, Avinash (1990), 'Growth Theory after Thirty Years', in Peter Diamond, ed., *Growth/Productivity/Unemployment, Essays to Celebrate Bob Solow's Birthday*, Cambridge, Mass.: MIT Press.

Dorfman, R., P.A. Samuelson and R.M. Solow (1958), *Linear Programming and Economic Analysis*, New York: McGraw-Hill.

Fisher, Franklin (1983), *Disequilibrium Foundations of Equilibrium Economics*, Cambridge: Cambridge University Press.

Fisher, Irving (1906), *The Nature of Capital and Income*, New York: Augustus M. Kelley.

Garegnani, Pierangelo (1976), 'On a change in the notion of equilibrium in recent work on value and distribution', in M. Brown, K. Sato and P. Zarembka, eds., *Essays in Modern Capital Theory*, Amsterdam: North-Holland, pp. 25–45. References are to the version reprinted in J. Eatwell and M. Milgate, eds. (1983), *Keynes's Economics and the Theory of Value and Distribution*. London: Duckworth, pp. 129–45.

Goodwin, Richard M. (1970), *Elementary Economics from the Higher Standpoint*, Cambridge: Cambridge University Press.

Goodwin, Richard M. and Lionello F. Punzo (1987), *The Dynamics of a Capitalist Economy*, Boulder, CO: Westview Press.

Hahn, Frank (1966), 'Equilibrium Dynamics with Heterogeneous Capital Goods', *Quarterly Journal of Economics*, **80**(4), November, pp. 633–46.

Hahn, Frank (1984), *Equilibrium and Macroeconomics*, Cambridge, Mass.: MIT Press.

Hodgson, Geoffrey M. (1988), *Economics and Institutions*, Cambridge: Polity Press.

Jevons, William Stanley (1911), *Theory of Political Economy*, 4th edition, ed. H. Stanley Jevons, London: Macmillan.

Kaldor, Nicholas (1972), 'The Irrelevance of Equilibrium Economics', *Economic Journal*, **82**, December, pp. 1237–55.

Leijonhufvud, Axel (1983), 'What was the Matter with IS-LM?' in J.P. Fitoussi, ed., *Modern Macroeconomic Theory*, Oxford: Basil Blackwell.

Marshall, Alfred (1890, 1920), *Principles of Economics*, 1st and 8th eds, London: Macmillan.

Morgenstern, Oskar (1972), 'Thirteen Critical Points in Contemporary Economic Theory: An Interpretation', *Journal of Economic Literature*, **10**, December, pp. 1163–89.

Nelson, R.R. and S.G. Winter (1982), *An Evolutionary Theory of Economic Change*, Cambridge, Mass.: Harvard University Press.

Rizvi, A. Abu Turab (1991), 'Specialization and the Existence Problem in General Equilibrium Theory', *Contributions to Political Economy*, **10**, pp. 1–20.

Samuelson, Paul (1967), 'Indeterminacy of Development in a Heterogeneous-Capital Model with Constant Saving Propensity', in Shell (1967), pp. 219–31.

Shell, Karl, ed. (1967), *Essays on the Theory of Optimal Economic Growth*, Cambridge, Mass.: MIT Press.

Sraffa, Piero (1960), *Production of Commodities By Means of Commodities, Prelude to a Critique of Economic Theory*, Cambridge: Cambridge University Press.

8 Krishna Bharadwaj and the revival of classical theory

Mark Knell and Sunder Ramaswamy

I Introduction

When asked to review Sraffa's *Production of Commodities by Means of Commodities* in 1962, Krishna Bharadwaj offered to write the review within 'a month or so'. Recognizing the importance of the book in reviving classical theory and re-evaluating marginal theory, she spent two years reading the original classical economists in depth. It was during this period that Krishna Bharadwaj had radically altered her 'theoretical perspective in economics',[1] laying the groundwork for a number of important and original essays on economic theory and economic development in the classical tradition. The review appeared in 1964, attracting attention from a number of scholars, including Piero Sraffa, because of its lucid style.

Krishna Bharadwaj began her review by placing Sraffa in the context of the history of economic thought:

> Economic theory has its fair share of conundrums. Discarded as mere 'chimeras' by the more pragmatic and empirically oriented economists, these puzzles continue to fascinate those with a flair for abstraction and challenge their speculative ingenuity. Of these, the 'chimera of absolute value', long fallen into oblivion after the unsuccessful efforts, notably by Ricardo and Marx, to discover an invariant yardstick to measure value, has now been revived [by] Piero Sraffa ...[2]

Sraffa solved the problem of the invariable measure of value that plagued Ricardo by introducing the standard commodity. There is another, more subtle, message contained in this passage that suggests that this solution is not only of historical interest, but one that revives an approach to economic theory discarded, in part, because of this problem. For both Krishna Bharadwaj and Piero Sraffa, the history of economic thought is not the cumulative progression of knowledge, but a history of knowledge that is often 'submerged and forgotten'[3] because of ideology, the historical context, or logical difficulties. Krishna made her case most strongly in the Dutt Lectures, where she argued against economic theory 'as a purely logical construction'. 'If this were true', she argued, 'the now dominant neoclassical theory would seem to be a higher stage in a sequential development of theory; and classical political economy, correspondingly, only a primitive effort at theorizing, interest-

107

ing only to the historian of ideas.'[4] She believed, like Sraffa, that classical political economy is not simply the precursor of the marginal approach, but a superior alternative to it.

Krishna Bharadwaj argued the superiority of the classical theory throughout most of her academic life. She took the position that classical theory and marginalist theory were alternative theories of value and distribution. Both theories dealt with the mutual interaction between production and exchange, but the classical approach is a theory of production and the marginalist approach is a theory of exchange. She maintained that the classical theory

> was constructed around the central concept of social surplus, modes of its appropriation, distribution and utilization characteristic of the relevant mode of production. The marginalist economic theory, on the other hand, was constructed around the concept of market equilibrium attained by the balancing of opposite and independent, symmetrically counterpoised forced of supply and demand.[5]

For Krishna Bharadwaj the classical theory of value and distribution becomes interesting when placed in the social context of a particular market form or mode of production. In this context the nature and extent of exchange and the degree of commercialization depend on the conditions of production and production relations. As Krishna points out 'In history ... it was only when the productive forces were accelerated within the economy that internal commerce could grow and make a larger and wider surplus produce available for external commerce as well.'[6] In the following two sections we consider the idea of Krishna Bharadwaj that classical theory is superior to marginalist theory because it allows for the variety and complexity of different market forms. It is through her clarification of the different market forms that can coexist simultaneously in the same economy that one can see the importance of her contribution toward reviving classical theory and in using this approach as a basis for an applied theory of production.

II   The revival of classical theory
Krishna Bharadwaj accepted the central question of classical political economy as the starting point for her work: 'On what does the general progress and wealth of a nation depend?'[7] For the classical economists the answer to this question depended on the amount of 'surplus' available. The notion of social surplus is the common thread around which one constructs the various arguments in classical political economy. This is only the starting point. In the Dutt Lectures, Krishna summarized the basic questions of classical political economy.

> (a) What does this surplus consist of and what determines its size? (b) Where does it originate? (c) Among whom is it distributed? (d) What determines its growth

over time? (e) What happens to the relative shares of surplus accruing to the different classes of revenue appropriators as the size of the surplus increases? How, in turn, do these distributive relations affect the process of accumulation?[8]

This set of questions goes beyond the notion of surplus and suggests that history is important to classical political economy. For Krishna the notion of social surplus, or the 'core' of classical theory, is independent of history leaving the more interesting questions of classical political economy as being historically specific. The reason for accepting the 'core' of classical theory is that the generation of surplus is important in all societies, whether primitive, slave, feudal, capitalist or socialist.[9] Questions explaining the data of the theory are outside the 'core' and historically specific.[10] The role of profits in capitalism, for example, depends on the institutions that define the capital market, and the idea of conflicting class interests depends on contracts and power relations. Institutions, social relations and the role of contracts become interesting in classical theory because they explain the data of the economic system. But at the same time they should not be confused with the 'core' of classical theory.

Krishna Bharadwaj argued for the superiority of classical theory over marginalist theory on the basis that it could consider a variety of complex social relations in a specific historical context. This was contrary to the prevailing view of Walras and Jevons who thought of the marginalist theory as a distinctly different and superior approach to classical theory because of its neat logical and analytical symmetry and the view of Alfred Marshall that the history of thought is a linear progression that allows new and superior ideas, such as marginalist theory, to supplant and, as Krishna Bharadwaj described it, to 'subvert' classical theory.[11] To obtain interesting results, marginalist theory requires 'well-behaved' price and quantity responses. This requires that the institutional framework and the behaviour of agents be specified in a certain way. As a consequence the marginalist approach is restrictive in its ability to incorporate the variety of historical conditions under which changes in output, methods of production, consumption and distribution take place. Eventually it was shown that a 'well-behaved' de-mand relationship for capital was inconsistent with the neat logical structure, severely limiting the ability of marginalist theory to consider problems of growth and accumulation.

The surplus-based approach allows for the variety and complexity of dif-ferent behaviours and institutional forms to influence the determination of production, consumption and distribution. In the classical approach prices are treated as compatible with the required circular reproduction of the system consistent with the rules regarding the generation, appropriation and distribu-tion of surplus. Institutions, such as 'contracts' and 'habits and customs', or other 'historically given circumstances' affect behaviour and therefore the ability to create wealth.[12] It was for these reasons that Krishna Bharadwaj stressed that it was not possible to discuss the process of accumulation independent of social and power relations.

III   Toward an applied theory of production
The rejection of the marginalist approach and her strong belief that social and power relationships underly 'the peculiarities of production and exchange processes'[13] led Krishna Bharadwaj to consider problems of economic development from the surplus-based approach. While all societies must produce a surplus to exist, the variety and complexity of different market forms in Indian agriculture posed an interesting problem for classical theory. Neither activity analysis or neoclassical production theory could look at 'the concrete conditions under which surplus is produced, appropriated and distributed'[14] because the 'relations among social classes do not enter the analysis of production, which is confined to the market decisions of individual producers.'[15] The variety and complexity of different behaviours and institutional forms present in different modes of production play an important role in determining 'the diversity of commercialization processes and their outcomes at different historical conjunctures.'[16] Inspired by Marx's simple characterization of the process of transition between different modes of production relations, Krishna maintained that the dynamics of change in Indian agriculture rest on the idea that multiple modes of production coexist and that these modes do not fit the pure categories characterized by Marx. This led her to the idea of interlinked markets.

Krishna Bharadwaj developed these themes in a study on the production conditions in Indian agriculture.[17] Written in response to neoclassical interpretations of a farm management study based on different centres, farm sizes and crops, she used the statistics to compare the production performance, input–utilization patterns across farms and regions, and the transaction terms of a differentiated peasant class. In this study, she classified the peasantry according to their access to land, as well as to the nature of exchange involvement in the agrarian situation where competitive capitalistic markets have not yet emerged. She also attempted to stratify peasants according to their status in production and their corresponding involvement in exchange under conditions of uneven commercialization.

Krishna Bharadwaj developed the idea of interlinked markets to explain the diversity of commercialization processes and the variety of different modes of production relations. The basic idea of interlinked markets is that two economic agents in an asymmetric power relationship interacting in two or more markets enter into a contract with interlinking terms. This phenomenon occurs in Indian agriculture when a landlord 'stipulates, as a part of the tenancy contract, attachment of labour services which are underpaid or un-paid.'[18] The power relationship between the landlord and tenant determine the tenurial conditions and consequently an interlinking exploitative process. At the same time, in the developing economies the process of commercializa-tion tends to occur more rapidly in output markets than in the labour, credit and land markets because of certain 'external' pressures created by the global market. The consequence of this structure of production and exchange is a process of uneven commercialization that affects 'the rate and pattern of reinvestment of surplus and hence, in turn the growth of surplus itself' in a way that reinforces the negative tendencies created in the global market.[19] Because, it is easy to undermine a development strategy when relatively more development markets coincide with less developed ones, Krishna sug-gests that 'policy design has to take account of the complex of activities'.[20]

Nevertheless, by her own admission, game theorists took over her idea of interlinked markets, although they used more formal analyses.[21] The key difference between the two approaches, however, is that the game theorists continued to ask the standard neoclassical static efficiency question and to explain the coexistence of different exchange systems rather than their transi-tions or their effects on the aggregate patterns of production and growth. In particular, Krishna Bharadwaj focused on the macrodynamics that the proc-esses of differentiation generated within the coexisting but interacting ex-change systems. Because her approach recognizes the variety and complexity of different behaviours and institutional forms as important to growth and accumulation, it may be her work parallels more closely the 'national system of innovation' approach pioneered by Freeman, Lundvall, and Nelson in the late 1980s.

What emerged out of her analysis of production conditions in India is neither the simple scenario of dualism (reflected in the agriculture–industry dichotomy), nor the dynamic advance of capitalistic accumulation drawn in the image of Britain. Indian agriculture is unique in that, despite substantial changes in GNP and its composition since the planning process in the early 1950s, no significant shift has occurred in the proportion of population de-pending on agriculture for bare survival or even in the numbers subsisting below the 'poverty line'.

Krishna Bharadwaj viewed classical theory as superior to the marginalist approach because it was more open and flexible to deal analytically with processes of differentiation of production, distribution and exchange. She developed a surplus-based applied theory of production in the context of India, inclusive of its colonial past and within changing international con-junctures. Undoubtedly, she combined the criticisms of marginalist approach and the revival of classical theory with the variety and complexity of market forms underlying the historical process of accumulation.

Notes

1. Born on 21 August 1935, Krishna Bharadwaj began formal study of economics in 1952. See her autobiographical entry in Philip Arestis and Malcolm Sawyer, eds, *A Biographical Dictionary of Dissenting Economists* (Edward Elgar, 1992).
2. K. Bharadwaj, 'Value through exogenous distribution', *Economic Weekly*, **24**, 1964, pp. 1450–54, reprinted in G.C. Harcourt and N.F. Laing, *Capital and Growth* (Penguin, 1971).
3. Preface to P. Sraffa, *Production of Commodities by Means of Commodities* (Cambridge University Press, 1960). See also K. Bharadwaj, *Classical Political Economy and Rise to Dominance of Supply and Demand Theories*, 2nd ed. (Sangam Books, 1986); hereafter referred to as *Classical Political Economy*.
4. *Classical Political Economy*, p. 4.
5. K. Bharadwaj, 'Production and Exchange in Theories of Price Formation and Economic Transition', in M. Baranzini and R. Scazzieri, *Foundations of Economics* (Blackwell, 1986), p. 339; hereafter *Production and Exchange*.
6. *Production and Exchange*, p. 354.
7. *Classical Political Economy*, p. 6.
8. *Classical Political Economy*, p. 6.
9. *Production and Exchange*, pp. 340–55.
10. The data of the core includes the social output, technology and the real wage. For a discussion of the 'core' of classical theory, see P. Garegnani, 'Value and Distribution in Classical Economists and Marx', *Oxford Economic Papers*, **36** (1984), pp. 291–325.
11. One of the most important contributions of Krishna Bharadwaj was to show how Alfred Marshall subverted classical theory by integrating marginalist methods into it. She focused on two problems in Marshall's work: (1) theoretical problems resulting from the integration of classical and marginal analysis; and (2) the argument of Marshall that the history of economic thought is cumulative progression of knowledge. See *Classical Political Economy* and K. Bharadwaj, *Themes in Value and Distribution* (Unwin Hyman, 1989).
12. *Classical Political Economy*, p. 35. Quotes are from Adam Smith, David Ricardo and Karl Marx, respectively.
13. *Production and Exchange*, p. 358.
14. *Production and Exchange*, p. 358.
15. *Classical Political Economy*, p. 73.
16. K. Bharadwaj, 'A Note on Commercialization in Agriculture', in K.N. Raj et. al., *Essays on Commercialization of Indian Agriculture* (Oxford University Press, 1985), p. 331.
17. K. Bharadwaj, *Production Conditions in Indian Agriculture* (Cambridge University Press, 1974).
18. *A Note on Commercialization*, p. 336.
19. *A Note on Commercialization*, p. 338.
20. *A Note on Commercialization*, p. 346.
21. See her autobiographical essay, *op. cit.*

Name index

Ayres, C.E. 76, 79

Barbon, Nicholas 4, 6
Berkeley, George 4, 6, 9
Bharadwaj, Krishna 93–7, 100–103, 107–11
Bieston, Roger 4
Binmore, Ken 47
Blaug, Mark 63, 66–7
Brown, Vivienne 18
Burmeister, Edwin 97–101

Carlisle, Janice 77
Cass, David 97
Child, Josiah 4, 6
Clark, Charles 31
Commons, John R. 89

Davenant, Charles 4
Deacon, John 2
Defoe, Daniel 4, 6, 9
Dixit, Avinash 97, 99–102
Dorfman, R. 98

Evensky, Jerry 18

Fisher, Irving 97
Franklin, Benjamin 5
Freeman, C. 111

Garegnani, Pierangelo 98
Goodwin, Richard M. 95

Hahn, Frank 101, 103
Heckscher, Eli F. 6
Hegel, G.W.F. 11
Heilbroner, Robert L. 18
Hemming, N. 4
Hodgson, Geoffrey M. 103
Hollander, Samuel 67
Hont, Istvan 18
Hume, David 4, 14

Ignatieff, Michael 18

Jevons, William Stanley 93, 109
Johnson, Harry 8
Johnson, Samuel 32

Kaldor, Nicholas 100–101, 103
Keynes, J.M. 95

Leijonhufvud, Axel 100, 103
Lewis, C.S. 32
Lindgren, Ralph J. 18

Macfie, A.L. 17, 23, 54–5
McNally, David 32
Malynes, Gerard 4–6
Marshall, Alfred 15, 93–4, 102–3
Marx, Karl 11, 93, 95–6, 107, 110
Meardon, Stephen 43, 47–54
Mill, Harriet Taylor 88
Mill, James 77–8
Mill, John Stuart 14, 69, 75–89, 93
Misselden, Edward 4, 6
Mitchell, B.R. 67
Morgenstern, Oskar 103

Nelson, R.R. 103, 111
North, Douglass C. 89
North, Dudley 4–5

Ortmann, Andreas 43, 47–54

Petty, William 4, 6–7
Pocock, J.G.A. 18
Postlethwayt, Malachy 4, 6
Punzo, Lionello F. 95

Raphael, D.D. 17, 23, 54–5
Rashid, Salim 55
Ricardo, David 13, 88–9, 93–4, 96, 107
Robinson, Joan 101
Rosenberg, Nathan 53
Rosen, Sherwin 53

Samuelson, Paul 98
Shell, Karl 97

Subject index

abilities, required for eductive strategy 48
abolition of poverty, reforms for 84–5
Abstract of British Historical Statistics 67
actual wage, bargaining and 67
'Adam Smith and Laissez Faire' 32
'Adam Smith and the Market Mechanism' 55
'Adam Smith problem' 44, 54–5
A Discourse of the Common Weal of this Realm of England (1549) 1, 3
analytical economist, Smith as 44, 54, 55–6
Ancient Logics 19
Ancient Physics 19–20
Anti-Corn Law League 13
Astronomy 18–19, 21–2, 35

Bengal, subsistence wages in 64
Bertrand game, technology as variable instead of price 52
British goods, protection for 14
British government (1820), free trade course 13
bundle of commodities, real wage and 103

Cambridge University, Kings College Research Centre 18
children
  inferior goods 72
  in the labour force 71
China
  stationary state of 37
  subsistence wages in 64–5
choices for firms, in game theoretic terms 52
churches 11, 81
classical economic policy 11–15
  differences from mercantilism 11
  Marshall and laissez faire 15
classical economists
  doctrine of natural order and 2

exceptions to principle of free exchange 1, 11
  as exponents of 'agrarian capitalism' 32
classical and marginalist theory, alternatives of value and distribution 108
classical theory
  argument of social surplus in 108–9
  natural prices and 94
  open questions about 102–3
  revival of 108–10
    'core' of 109
    social surplus in 108–9
  superiority over marginalist theory 109
  theory of 'givens' in 102
classical theory of rent, mathematically based 93
classical theory of value and distribution, in context of particular market form 108
'clubs and cabal', applications of principle of partial spectator 23
coal miners, Smith discussing 34
'commodius use' (utility), price and 5
'conducted by nature' 19
'Considerations Concerning the First Formation of Languages' 20–21
Considerations on the East-India Trade (1701) 5
Corn Laws, controversy over 13

demand, cross-elasticity of 6
demand and supply curves in Stage A, short run and 70
demand and supply equilibrium-based theory *see* DSE-based theory
distribution of property, conditions for 80
'Distribution of wealth', 'a matter of institutions solely' 75
diversity of commercialization processes, interlinked markets and 110

of the evolution of moral sentiments
48
the generalized 58–9
payoffs 45–8, 58–60
result in Pareto-efficient outcomes 43
of self-command acquisition 46–7
WN and incentive-compatible state
intervention 49–50
social surplus, argument in classical
theory 108–9
specific propensity, partial spectator 23–
4
Stage B, supply and demand shifts in 71
state intervention, incentive-compatibil-
ity of 49–50, 53, 55–6
stoicism
basis of 18–19, 26
design in the universe 20
human nature of natural propensities
in 19
review of recent literature 17–18
Stoic model, completed in *Astronomy* 21
stoic thought
determinism of 20, 25
EPS and 18–23
implications of 23–5
importance of language in 21
oikeiosis in 19
Studies in Words 32
subsistence theory of wages, demand
curve and 68
subsistence wages
Bengal 64
China 64–5
supply and demand shifts, in Stage B 71
'supposed' impartial spectator 23
'surplus' available, general wealth and
progess and 108
surplus-based, versus DSE-based theory
93
surplus-based theory
what it should include 94
what this approach allows for 109–10
system of natural liberty, man and
systematic entropic effect of 25
system stability, importance in Smith's
system 24

technological advances, working-class
and 86

technological change
DSE-based theories and 103
long-period 'natural' prices and 102
technology
'best practice' technique and 102
and production process 52, 83
specification of development 103
'The Dialogic Experience of Conscience: Adam Smith and the
Voices of Stoicism' 18
The Nature of Capital and Income 97
theory of production
towards an applied 110–11
interlinked markets in 110
'The Scottish Tradition in Economic
Thought' 17
The state, as a super-institution 80
*The Theory of Moral Sentiments see
TMS*
TMS 17–19, 22–5
acquisition of self-command in 44–7
actions motivated by sympathy 54
basic incentive problem 55
loanable funds theory in 66
Man yesterday and 46
model of acquisition of self-command
in 47, 54
model of human behaviour in 22
and Newtonian view of the world 48
relationship to *WN* 43
reputational enforcement and 49
Smith game and incentive problems
44, 54
struggles between two 'selves' 44
on subsistence wages 65
towards an applied theory of production
110–11
trigger strategy, in games 60
truck system, prohibition of 11
'Two Concepts of Morality: Adam
Smith's Ethics and its Stoic Origin'
18
two 'selves', 'Man Yesterday' and the
'Man Today' 44–5
two theories, value and distribution and
93–5

usury laws, business loans and 12
utilitarianism
Mill and 14–15